`MW01225678`

To Luis & Candace
What a joy meeting you
has been. I hope the information
here goes some way to
ensuring you life lives you
really would want to
live.
Love always
Tom Grbich

Dedication

This book is dedicated to:
The millions of people in the world, who know they deserve more out of life but (until now), didn't know how to get it.

The good friends from the Australia, Canada, New Zealand, the US, and the UK who wouldn't leave me alone until I wrote this, and

To my Mum (no longer with us) who was perhaps the "feistiest" person I've known.

Acknowledgements

It is also important to acknowledge all the great teachers in my life who contributed both consciously and unconsciously, to the creation of this "manual."

The Grand Master – Wong Lum was my greatest inspiration – it was he, who showed me that I was not born useless at all, and started me on my journey to joy.

I have learned, and continue to learn from my wife Susan, my children Lahia and Jaron, my friends Bryan Wild, Chris Dobson, Dean and Kathi Blazek, Kathy Dooley, Taron Puri, and Will Black, in particular; but every new person I meet brings new learning opportunities, and I am grateful to have each of them in my life.

Special thanks also go to Judy, Curtis, Sherrill, Will, Dean and Kathi for their contributions in proof reading this document.

Be not concerned for the child who is afraid of the dark, the real tragedy is the adult, who is afraid of the light. Originator unknown.

What People Say

Tom is a bright spot of clarity in an otherwise "iffy" world. I appreciate you on so many levels my "healing with love" friend - J. Dooley

Because of your teaching my life is totally different and my life with my wife is so peaceful and starting to be filled with LOVE. I enjoy LIVING LIFE Thanks for being part of that - D. Blazek

The Live The Life YOU Want" program (on which this book is based) has changed my life in many ways. Tom presented the course in such a way that every topic related to me as if I was the only one in the room, but at the same time, you felt you wanted to share your feelings with the group.

It was a great experience and I will always be ever grateful for meeting Tom—Linda

I was already a very positive person when I began the Live The Life YOU Want program but I had no idea as to how much of life I was still overlooking. I am so sorry that most of the others on the program had to wait forty or more years for it – I am only 19 and I just can't imagine how much better my life is going to do be now.
Tim

I remember how it was with me when you taught the Strive Program and the boost to my morale that it gave me - mostly due to your instruction. I walked away from there feeling I could lick the world and my self esteem well intact. I've never forgotten that experience.
Judy O

Contents

Title

INTRODUCTION

I am about to share some very personal information with you for one reason only. That reason is - to show you that how you **end** your life has nothing (necessarily), to do with how you **started** it. It all comes down to "you."

My father was primarily a physical abuser; my mother was the mental/emotional abuser. We lived on a small farm in an evil little place in the far North of New Zealand where no one could hear your screams, and if they did, "they'd mind their own business" – it wasn't "right" to concern yourself with the affairs of others.

> How you **END** your life has nothing (necessarily) to do with how you **STARTED** it – it all comes down to **"YOU."**
>
> *Tom Grbich*

My father could raise cuts on a bull's hide with a whip, and he could cut clean through a pair of corduroy trousers with a leather belt. If he wasn't beating me it seemed, my mother would either be telling me: I should have died at birth, I was "born useless," or asking why I didn't just run away from home and never come back.

As kids coming home from school, my sister and I would stop at the old plum tree down below the house, to listen for World War III. If there was a battle going on, self preservation meant sneaking carefully into our rooms via the back door, so as not to be involved.

Two things set me on the "right" path in my life. The first was when I couldn't bring myself to pull the triggers of a shotgun, to blow my brains out, at the grand age of eight. I had had an encounter with **both** parents that had gone on for about two hours, and had decided to prove that although I **may** have been born useless, I wasn't **entirely** useless – I at least had the courage to do something about it.

When I couldn't pull those triggers - no matter how hard I tried, I experienced my first total emotional meltdown. I don't ever remember crying so hard because in my child's mind, that was the final proof that they were right. I was **so** damned useless that I couldn't even do the one thing I had the power to do, that would have ended the pain!

At that point I had to accept that whatever happened in my life from there on - I deserved. By my inability to pull that trigger, I had forfeited my whining and blame rights.

The second thing occurred the day I left home. On that day I remember "saying to myself" that my mother and father had no further control over me, and would not be allowed to influence anything in my life – **ever** again.

The combined result of these two gifts of learning was to ensure that I never complained – life is tough so – "get on with it," and... I took personal **responsibility,** for everything I did from there on.
However inappropriately arrived at, those two events were my saviours.

Many of you who read this may have had better lives (I certainly hope so), and some of you may have had worse. Whatever the case, until you are ready to:

~ Quit whining and feeling sorry for yourselves, **and**

~ Take (**full**) responsibility for your life, **you are not ready to move on**.

If you are not ready to move on then **don't try,** because you'll only be setting yourself up for another perceived failure, and no one needs that. I recommend that you don't read another page until you are absolutely **sure** that you are ready to **commit** to your new life, **and,** to take full responsibility for you, your actions, and your behaviour from here on. If you can't do that, this will become just "another book you've read, that didn't work." It will be the "book's" fault, and your never-ending search will continue.

Take your time
It is also incredibly important that you read this book and do the exercises **at your own pace**. It is **not** a race or a competition – you should be prepared to go over a section as many times as you need

until it makes sense to you, and come back and do things again, if you find your views changing along the way.

What you have to understand **right now** is that your life as it **has** been, **is**, and will **continue** to be, has **nothing to do with this book** (or any **other** book for that matter). The truth is that **no** book, course, or counsellor can change you **or** your life - only **YOU** can do that. This manual will give you all the tools that most people will ever need to be able to turn their lives around - but only **YOU** - **applying** those tools daily, can make it work.

While I cannot believe that **everything** we face in this lifetime is of our choosing, I **do** believe that at least as much as 90% of it is. Maybe the other 10% is also our choice - made at a level beyond our consciousness. I won't argue that, but the aim of this manual is to provide you with the tools to take control of the choices that **are** conscious, and to change the quality of your life in the process.

What vs. how?

Interestingly, I managed to put off creating this program for nearly twenty years – during which time friends and acquaintances in New Zealand had been pressing me to "do something" like this. But I couldn't see any point. Shelves are sagging under the weight of personal development programs all over the world – why create another?

As pressure started to build again shortly after moving to Canada, the answer finally came. A friend in New Zealand who had done some of the best programs around, told me... "I found very quickly that these programs were excellent at telling me **'what'** I needed to do, but when I asked **"how"** they all ran for cover. In the 18 years that I've known you, you've always had the 'how' - so you **have** to write that book."

Of course we **will** be looking at "what" you need to be doing in order to move ahead, but if I don't also give you the **tools** to change (and instructions on how to **use** those tools), then I will have done little (if anything) to help you.

My philosophy is that if I find you dying of thirst in the desert and tell you **what** you need to do (dig three feet down and you'll find water e.g.) but I don't provide you with the tools to do that – then all I've done really, is to frustrate you.

If I tell you what to do and provide you with the latest well boring machine (the tool) but don't teach you how to use it – then I **still** haven't helped you. Sure you might figure it out for yourself, but you might not too.

So the overriding objective of this book is to assist you to discover **what** you need to do, provide you with **tools** that will help you to facilitate the job **and**, teach you how to use them.

Tools
Regarding tools, it's important to note that this is intended to be both a book **and** a manual. Reading the book without doing the work will no doubt provide interesting reading - but if you are **serious** about changing your life, then applying the tools to some of the work prepared for you, will be **critical** to achieving that goal.

Note that there are documents to be supplied separately from the book so that you can print them, including some of those important tools that will assist tremendously in helping you to achieve your goals. Unfortunately, the publishers are unable to include a CD with the book at this time so you will need to get your downloadable files via email.

For the North American "letter" size please send an email to ltlyw+letter@tomgrbich.com

For the European "A4" size, please address your email to... ltlyw+a4@tomgrbich.com

You do not need to put anything in the subject line or write a request. On receipt of your email, the files will automatically be sent to you.

They include:

~   Personal Evaluation questionnaires x 3 (one to start, another midway through the program, and one at the end)

~   A Draft Action Plan

- ~ A "Needs" Chart
- ~ A Personal Life Chart
- ~ A "Things To Work On page"
- ~ An "Attitudes Working For You" form
- ~ A "Final Action Plan"
- ~ A "Getting The Most" questionnaire
- ~ A "Personal Discoveries" page, and
- ~ Stories that will compliment and accentuate the chapter that you are working with at any given time.

As you go through the manual you will be guided to open the appropriate tool or story – please don't open them until guided, as you'll lose the intended impact if you do.

Self Evaluation

This is a very personal questionnaire where you rate yourself and your world as you see things, at that point in time. It will become perhaps the most powerful tool of the whole program.

Draft Action Plan
The Draft Action Plan is intended to get you started on moving towards a Final Action Plan, which will ultimately change your life. As you go through the program you will enter items that are important to you, **and commit to doing something about them**. This is the plan to get you started, on changing the rest of your life.

Personal Life chart
The Personal Life Chart provides a graphic representation of where you see your life right now, from a bunch of perspectives. It is also very powerful – showing you exactly where your life needs the most improvement.

Getting the most page
This page is a questionnaire aimed at assisting you to get the most out of the program. It is important to answer the questions honestly.

Needs chart

10

Unfulfilled needs are one of the greatest causes of stress in life. **Understanding** your needs and the needs of others, will be a huge help towards attaining your goal of living the life **you** want.

Personal Discoveries

The "Personal Discoveries" sheet is provided as a place for you to note down any "things about yourself," your life or your environment that you...

~ Hadn't realised (or maybe hadn't thought about)

~ That **need** to be changed, or

~ Maybe are just "nice things to know," about yourself, and how you came to be the person you are.

Things To Work On

"Things To Work On" is the place for you to take notes of any special things that you want to work on personally (but which may not be a priority), that you discover as you go along.

Final Action Plan

By the end of the manual you should have already completed some of the important tasks on your **Draft Action Plan**, and you should now be in a position to be much more specific about what you want to achieve from here on. You may also want to re-prioritise those things remaining on the **Draft Action Plan**. The **Final Action Plan** is the place to do this. This is the plan that you will "live" with.

Summing up

So to sum up... the primary objective of this manual is to inspire **you,** to make **your** life, whatever **you** want it to be. It will achieve this by...

~ Providing practical **tools**, to give you an opportunity to live the life **YOU** want, that are **real**.

~ Providing practical **ideas** (that you can modify or use as they are, in your own life).

~ Offering **techniques** that you can use to deal with those stress-creating issues of life.

~ Generating some **lasting excitement** for you by putting **real hope** back in your life, and

~ Going **beyond** telling you "**what**" you can do with your life. Our most important objective is to help you discover **how** to do it – in ways that work for you.

It is very likely that you will find this to be an extremely comprehensive "manual," and I therefore recommend that you take it in "chunks" that work for you (a couple of pages or a chapter a week for example), and be prepared to repeat sections, or even the whole book, as often as you need to.

Working through it in "chunks" is extremely important in fact – because it gives you time to absorb what you have just learned, and to sincerely contemplate what it means, with regard to where you go from here.

Chapter 1

GETTING STARTED

The Manual

Important note: While there will be some inevitable "crossover" throughout the book, the first part is aimed at getting you organised, and helping you to understand why you may not have done as much with your life as you think you should have.

The second part is aimed at providing the tools to change your life, and the encouragement to do something about it.

(Another) **Important note:** I cannot stress strongly enough, the importance of appreciating that everything in this world is just somebody else's perception. So nothing in this book is either "right" or "wrong" – it's just "my perception." My recommendation therefore, is that you set aside the things that you don't immediately relate to and come back to them periodically. You'll be surprised at how perceptions can change, with new information.

> Everything in this world is just somebody else's perception – the **only** "reality," is **yours**.
>
> *Tom Grbich*

The very first thing I want you to do is to print the **Draft Action Plan** and address the "Responsibility" aspect.

Note that you will need Adobe Reader to open it and this program can be obtained free from http://www.adobe.com/

Feel free to use your own words but what you need to write here is something like... "I take personal responsibility for **at least 90%** of what happens in my life, from (today's date) on" (no more whining).

Next to 'Commitment' I want you to write something like... "I commit **100%**, to doing everything that I put in this plan."

It's important to understand that anything less than 100% is **not good enough**. By way of an example, a study in the US in 1995 (yes that's 19**95**) showed that in the US alone, if 99.**9**% was good enough then...

- ~ 22,000 cheques would have been deducted from the wrong bank accounts **every hour**
- ~ 1,324 telephone calls would have been misplaced **every 60 seconds**
- ~ 12 babies would have been given to the wrong mothers **every day**
- ~ 2,268,500 faulty tyres would have been shipped, and
- ~ More than 20,000 incorrect drug prescriptions would have been given out that year

Is **your future** worth better than a 99.9% commitment? You bet it is!

And the question is – if you're not willing to make this level of commitment to **yourself**, then what **are** you willing to commit to?

Print the **Personal Life Chart** and being brutally honest, mark exactly where you see yourself right now. This could perhaps then go on your refrigerator door to remind you of the areas that are holding you back and can also be a measure of progress, as you change the positions over time.

Print the **Personal Evaluation-01** and being equally honest, fill it out. Once you have done this, you should **put it in a sealed envelope**, and we will come back to it at an appropriate time later on.

Power of the mind
One of the most important things for you to appreciate is that wherever you are in your life right now – **you got there via your thinking**. Everything in this life comes down to **how** we think and for most people – life, circumstances, observations, and other people, have taught us **what** to think.

That doesn't mean it's right – it's just the way it is.

The Belief / Attitude cycle

When we're born, we don't have any particular thoughts or therefore, attitudes, (although some parents might argue that) about anything – but, we learn very quickly. Learning comes from information, which in turn comes (mostly) from observing and/or doing things, and seeing what result we get.

As per the diagram, this **information** forms the basis of our **beliefs**. Out of our beliefs come our **attitudes**, out of our attitudes come **behaviours**, out of our behaviours we get **results** (or **consequences**), which either confirm or deny our earlier information – and so the cycle goes on...

It's important to appreciate though, that it is not just **information** that is the basis of our beliefs – it is even more so, our **interpretation** of that information!

Using the diagram, let's say that the **information** I have been given all my life, is that blondes are **bad** people.

Because I have no reason not to trust the source/s of that information – that becomes my **belief** – blondes are **bad** people.

My **attitude** towards blondes is likely to be something along the line of... "maybe blonde babies should be terminated at birth."

And with an attitude like that you can appreciate that my **behaviour** around blondes is not going to be especially pleasant; with the **result**, that I probably get popped on the nose fairly regularly by them – confirming my information (that blondes are bad people), and strengthening my beliefs, attitudes and so on.

Then one day with my car broken down at the side of the road, I watch brunettes' etc drive on by the dozen, until finally who should stop? You got it – a blonde.

With my car repaired, I drive down the road evaluating this **new information**. Out of this information comes a **modified *belief***... "well maybe not **all** blondes are bad."

My ***attitude*** shifts to considering that maybe at least **some** of them should be allowed to live. My ***behaviour*** improves around blondes with a resulting fewer pops on the nose, confirming my new ***information*** and... so it goes.

Let's bring that closer to home...

~ Your earliest ***Information*** is that you were born useless, and you will never amount to anything

~ Out of that comes the ***Belief*** (typically) that you really have no right to be here, (and all the problems that go with that thought, begin)

~ Your ***Attitude*** is that "if you are born useless, there is no hope - you can't go and get "reborn," and if you are fated to be a bum, there's no point in being an educated one, so you don't work hard at school

~ Your ***Behaviour*** becomes progressively aggressive and defensive. You "hate yourself," and either you fight every one and every thing around you; you submit - accepting whatever people want to do to you as "the way it is" – you "deserve it," or, you try to "escape" in a world of alcohol, drugs, or whatever.

~ The **Results** include people avoiding you, teachers confirming that you're stupid... (confirming your '***Information***') and the cycle goes on.

Then someone comes into your life who cares, and they take the time to find a way to prove to you that **no one** is born useless – that we are **taught** to believe that, and **anything** we've been taught – **we can be taught to change**.

With that **new *Information*** (that you were **not** born useless), you begin to believe that perhaps **everything** in life can change – **if** you are willing to allow it, and **if** you're prepared to **drive** it.

Appreciate that **everyone deals with information differently** – sometimes because we **see** things differently. How **you** see the information you receive will have a **huge** effect on how you deal with it, and how you **deal** with your information will always ultimately, determine what does, or does not change for **you**.

The point is?

The point is – your beliefs, attitudes, and behaviours will **continue to provide the exact results they were intended to provide** (intentionally or otherwise) – until you **change** your information **AND/OR,** how you **"see"** that information**!**

This is critically important – far too often we see things as **we** are rather than as **they** are. As an example – you're walking home late one night and it starts to rain. You've been told never to take the short cut because some seriously bad people hang out there, but you haven't heard of anyone being mugged for some time, so you decide to take the risk. Then – half way through, you hear a drink can rattle behind you and what goes through your mind? Your perception (and therefore your reality) is probably going to look something like this... "Oh my God – I'm going to get what I deserved – I was so **stupid** I **knew** I shouldn't take this route...

You "see" yourself being beaten up – maybe raped or killed, and you curse yourself over and over for having been so stupid. Then you turn around to face your fate and find a little kitten in the rubbish bin you just passed, looking down at the can he knocked out. Do you think this new information might change your perceptions? I think so too.

It's interesting how differently two people can see the same information. For example, let's say that with no agenda and no strings attached, I make the simple statement "I just wanted to say that you are an absolutely beautiful person" to a young lady sitting beside me. One young lady might be thrilled and heart-warmed by the sincerity of the compliment – another may think I'm a dirty old man, trying to "hit on her." Every aspect of the information presented, was the same to both - but the "message" taken **from** it, was worlds apart.

So, for **any** positive, lasting change to take place in **your** life, you need to be willing to **receive** and **modify** your current information, and thereby change your beliefs. **Nothing** can change in your life until you are willing to do that.

This Is the challenge of this program – to provide you with enough information (that you are willing to believe in); to empower you to dump your **old** information, and thereby change your life.

In December 2005 I cheated death by restoring ten inches (30 Cm) of dead colon.   The walls were disintegrating, blood was seeping through, and it was too far-gone to be operable.   The information given to me was, "There is nothing left that we can do for you – in five to seven days the wall will disintegrate completely, and you will bleed to death in about two and a half minutes."

I chose to "see" the information differently – I saw it instead as, "You have a physical challenge that will take you beyond anything you previously thought possible – if you are willing to meet it."   The obvious alternative was death.

Aboriginals in many parts of the world will die if they believe they have been cursed by a witch doctor, and nothing in the book of modern medicine can save them.

And look at Forrest Gump (if you haven't seen the movie – go see it – it carries a message that compliments this program tremendously) – he just didn't realise that he was "too dumb" to be successful. The **information** he received from his Mum all his life was that he could do anything – so he did...

Print the **Things To Work On page** (because today is as good as any day, to get moving) and note down...

~ What combination of information and beliefs has brought **you** to where you are now?

~ Is this information something that you would like to change?

~ If there are obstacles, are they a **result** of the information you have received, or is it more do with how you have "**seen**" that information?

~ What are you going to **do** about this, and

~ When do you plan to **start**?

The following poem "He Can" is a great one to add to your fridge billboard, but may I suggest rewriting it and replacing the "He" with

18

an "**I**."

HE CAN

If you think you are beaten - you are

If you think you dare not - you don't

If you like to win but you think you can't

It's almost certain you won't

If you think you'll lose - you're lost

For in all of this world we find

Success begins with a person's will

It's all in the state of your mind

If you think you're outclassed you are

You've got to think high to rise

You've got to be sure of yourself

Before you'll ever win the prize

Life's battles do not always go

To the stronger or faster man

But sooner or later the man who wins

Is the one who thinks he can.

Author unknown

There's a critically important saying that goes... "If you continue to do what you've always done - you'll continue to get what you've always got." It's often referred to as the "ultimate insanity – "continuing to do the same thing, and expecting a different result."

People wonder why they get the same problems in relationship after relationship, and yet the answer is quite simple. If you want things to change in your life, then most times, the **first** thing that needs to change - is the way **you** - think, and act.

There is an extremely important distinction here – you are not trying to change "**you**" – just the way you **think.**

When you change the way you think (or see things) your behaviour will change too, and that is the whole point.

Quote: *"Nature gave us two ends - one to think with, and the other to sit on. Since the beginning of time, our success or failure has been dependent on the one we use most." (Originator unknown)*

Your thinking/beliefs will be a prison that there is no escape from, or they will be your own personal rocket ship to your future - it all depends on you. (Tom Grbich)

Proceeding from here:

Much of what we're going to cover, you may feel you already know, or at least understand at some level. So what? That is very likely true, but the fact that you're reading this, suggests that there's still something missing wouldn't you agree?

My approach where someone has not been performing to his or her potential has always been similar to addressing the problem of a balloon that is sitting below the waterline. The required performance is that the balloon sit on **top** of the water so what do we do? We pump more air (training, counselling, or coaching) in and if we're lucky, the balloon might pop free - or it might just pop.

If we had taken the time to look a little deeper, we would have noticed that the **real** problem was that the cord was caught, and all we **really** needed to do was to **cut** it. And so it is with life. So often we get hooked up on "what needs to be pumped in" when all that was **really** needed, was for something to be taken out of the way. **Your** "cord" will be the information that you are basing your beliefs on and somehow, we have to get **you** to recognise it, and cut it.

What holds **people** back is not always so obvious, but the concept is really no different. In one of my training roles for a major corporation, a Sales Manager spoke to me about a staff member who was not performing. She was bright; she had joined the company on leaving school, and she had been one of the top performers in the customer service area before moving to sales, where she was failing miserably.

She had already been through the company's excellent training program, and she knew the products and services implicitly.

On spending some time with her I quickly confirmed that she did **not** need anything else "pumped in" (further "training"). Her territory was the East Coast of the North Island of New Zealand, which was renowned for **always** being in "hard times." When she called her prospects they would give her the age-old story of how they were "already almost out of business," they were "broke," and "if they spent any money on her products and services, it would just hasten their demise."

So what was it that was **really** holding her back? Only one thing - her thinking! And where did her thinking come from? From the **information** she was being given by her prospects.

She was an incredibly ethical young lady, and there was just no way that she was going to hasten her client's demise by **selling** them something – even at the cost of her job.

In the course of our discussion, I told her about some of the problems **I** had had when starting my first business, and asked if any of her services might have helped me. As the discussion progressed, she began to realise that she could actually **help** her customers in the same way that she would have helped me, and suddenly, what she had seen as doing "**to**" her customers became doing "**for**."

The shift was so subtle – doing "to" as opposed to doing "for," but she went back to those phones with a vengeance. Her belief now, was that she had an **obligation** to sell (in order to **save** her customer's businesses), and she was not taking "no" for an answer - from **anyone**. She quickly became the top selling Account Manager by such a margin, that her closest competitor was achieving only **half** of her target.

New information allied, to the power of **thinking** and **belief** changed her behaviour completely and the **result**, was that she began to perform at the top which she always should have been doing. Letters from at least two of her customers thanking her for refusing to back down because she had transformed their businesses, confirmed her information and her new belief that she really **was** working for the good of her customers – not the detriment.

The hardest sale

The hardest sale you will ever make - will typically be to **yourself**. Via this "manual" I hope to sell **you** the belief that if you learn the tools well enough and make them yours, you will have all the skills you need to then sell **yourself,** on the fact that **YOU CAN** change everything in your life - by changing the way you think and act. The way you act almost **always** stems from how you think. It all starts there.

It's important to understand that your ego will do all it can to get in your way, but the (coming) chapter on that nasty little rodent will help you to at least get it in check.

I can do this?? You **bet!!**

Exercise:
1. Review your worksheets and ensure they are up to date

2. Check that they accurately indicate what you are going to start doing, that they have timelines on them, and

3. Each day, or at **least** once a week − check to see what you actually **have** done, that you said you were going to do.

Chapter 2

GETTING THE MOST

There will be a bunch of things that will line up to stop you from getting the most out of this program (**all** of them ego based), but none will be more effective, than the JRB process. When things go wrong (and you can have tremendous fun watching people do this from here on), the JRB process comes into action with blinding speed...

J=Justify – you've got so many other things on your mind it's just impossible to concentrate

R=Rationalise – besides – it's really not that important to you – you only bought the book because Susie pestered you into it, and

B=Blame – the information is absolutely useless – you'd have to be a professor to understand it, the author couldn't teach a five-year-old to get an ice-cream to its mouth if his life depended on it... and so on

It's true – the next time something goes wrong at work (or wherever) just watch how quickly this process gets started. And sometimes, people actually **jump** the process going directly to blame!

Objective

By the end of this chapter you will be able to list:
  ~ The things that will attempt to stand in **your** way

  ~ What you can (personally) do to avoid those things, and

  ~ Relate in your own words the importance of recognising that there are **lots** of "small" things but how cautious we must be, before classifying them as "insignificant"

So to help ensure that you do get the most possible out of the program, what I want to do right now, is to talk about cars.

You didn't **know** that this was going to be about cars – wow – you really **do** have some work to do don't you?

Actually I'm only **partly** kidding - what is a car, really? It's a vehicle for getting you from one place to another right - from where you **are** to where you **want to be**? And I'm pretty sure that's what this program is supposed to be all about isn't it - getting from where you are now, to where you want to be? Great - so let's talk about cars then.

Tell me – have you ever owned a car that took you wherever you wanted to go - all by itself? No? So what part did **you** have to play? Oh yeah - you have to **drive** it!

And the same is true of this program. If I gave you the most expensive Ferrari you can buy, I'm sure you'd agree that it would probably be good for more than 300kph. And how do we **know** that? We know it because it has been **tested** at that speed.

But if your belief is that you can't be trusted with **driving** an expensive (ridiculously fast) car like that - how fast is it going to go now? It may not even get out of the garage (somebody might scratch it - right)? So a skateboard would be of more real use to you wouldn't it?

If you're not willing to test **yourself**, how will you ever know, what **you** are good for? That Ferrari that so impresses us doesn't even come **close** to what **you** are capable of. And if you **did** decide to test the Ferrari to see for **yourself** what it could do – you'd probably want to hire a racetrack for the day - with no other vehicles around and with lots of safety barriers etc. in place in case you 'lost it' - yes? You **need** a safe place for testing - and this is **your** safe place - to begin discovering what **you** are capable of!

This manual will provide you with a vehicle that no car on planet earth can match, but if you don't take it on and drive it. **Nothing... will... happen!**

One of the most frustrating, most meaningless, most useless words in the whole of the English language on its own; would have to be the word "potential."

Potential is nothing more than a puff of smoke - a dream, until you actually **do** something with it!

That little farm we lived on was miles from nowhere and one day the most exciting thing in **years** occurred. This big truck loaded with bags of fertiliser chugged up the hill past our house and began unloading right outside the gate. Mum blew a fuse (she **knew** something) but my father painted a picture of hills covered in lush grass, happy cows producing **way** more milk for sale and so on.

Both were right – the fertiliser **did** have the **potential** to increase grass growth dramatically and thereby, milk production – that was **proven** as the stack slowly melted down into the earth and the grass around it grew ten feet tall. It became our favourite play-place

Did it increase milk production though? No – you see the potential only became reality when it was taken out of the sack and spread around – and Mum **knew** that was never going to happen!

Is that where **your** potential lies too? When are you going to take **it** out of the sack?

It is **so** important to understand that you are what you think (or) believe you are. After I wrote my first sales training program, I decided to run it for private individuals who did not see themselves as sales people, but saw value in learning some sales skills.

> You are what you **think** you are. You can only **change** what you are, by changing your thinking.
>
> *Tom Grbich*

One of the people who attended the course was a 62-year-old lady called Jean. She was a totally dependable student until the final weeks of the course, when she didn't turn up at all.

She arrived for the final day however, and a little embarrassed, accounted for her absence. She told us that her life's dream had been to be a Real Estate Sales Person. Her family though, had always laughed and ridiculed her any time she suggested it, and she felt stupid for even thinking about it.

The program changed her information however, along with the belief that she could do it; and in those last few weeks she had been studying for and passed, her final exams!

Ok now let's look a little more closely at that car. How many cars have you ever owned where there wasn't a single thing you would have changed if you could?"

Let's say you don't like the console - so you rip that out, don't like the shape of the lights so you take them off, the shape of the hood isn't quite right so that goes, don't like the wheels, the door handles etc. What happens to the usefulness and/or the performance capabilities of the car?"

> There is only one reality in this world
> **– YOURS!**
>
> *Tom Grbich*

The car might not be perfect, but it was designed as an integral package, and so it is with this program. There will be sections that you don't feel are quite so 'important' or 'relevant' to you, or even that you maybe won't like – but they're **part of the whole** - so don't miss the real opportunity that the program provides, because of one part that doesn't "fit" so well with you (remember the JRB trap?).

Another thing that is critically important is to accept that there is only **one reality** in this world at any given time, and that is yours. That does **not** mean that you're right. Your reality is derived from your personal beliefs, and it can rule your life and your relationships. The great news however is that because you can **change** what you believe - it stands to reason that you can also therefore - change your reality.

My "reality" was that I was "born useless" and how do you change that? All my life I had heard this and who would know this better than your own mother? I rated myself about amoeba on the scale of life until my martial art teacher finally showed me that that was not true. He convinced me that I had been taught to **believe** that I was useless, and "anything that you've been taught – you can be taught to change" (remember?). I will never forget that day, because **that** was the day that I moved from existing - to living.

Earlier we discussed the power of the mind in healing – in fact, your mind is every **bit** as powerful in holding you back, **or** moving you forward. My mind held me back for 19 years – that's right it was **not** my upbringing, **not** my parents, not even my teachers. What held me back was my willingness to make their statements "my" reality but since I took the handbrake off, my new thinking has driven me like a Ferrari, and it continues to do so.

Some of the things that stand in the way of the progress of **anyone** doing programs like this include:

~ **Attitude** - deciding you "don't like me," you "don't like what I am saying," or you convince yourself that you "already know all of this"

~ **Fear** – the biggest obstacle that anyone will face in (and throughout) their lifetime

~ **Self consciousness** – you hold back because other people might laugh at you or think you're stupid (just another form of fear)

~ **Ego** – you try to convince yourself that you're just fine the way you are (so how come you're not happy then?)

~ Listening for what you **expect** to hear, instead of what I'm actually saying

~ Etc.

Exercise: If you have not done this before – count the number of "f's" in the following statement. Do it once only, try not to take more than 20 seconds, and write the number down.

"FINISHED FILES ARE THE RESULT OF YEARS OF SCIENTIFIC STUDY, COMBINED WITH THE EFFECTS OF THE EXPERIENCE OF MANY YEARS."

How many did you get - 3 or less, 4, 5, 6? More than 6? Ok 9 is actually the correct number. If you have done this before and got it right this time, try to remember how you fared the first time you did it.

Was this difficult? Of course it wasn't; yet you might be surprised to know that almost no one **ever** gets it right first time. What's the point? It's astonishing don't you think - that we had that incredibly simple little sentence **right in front of us** - we even **knew** what we were looking for, and yet we **still couldn't see it**!

So, do I have your agreement that if we can't see something that's right in front of our eyes, then chances are excellent that there are a whole bunch of **other** things out there - **right in front of us**, that we aren't seeing in **life** right now? Yes? And what about the things that **aren't** so obvious - that **aren't** right in front of our eyes? Uh oh!

Quote: *We tend to see what we* **expect** *to see.* A great example of this is standing at the cupboard looking for a jar that is right in front of us. We can't "see" it however because the one in front of us has a red label, and we were expecting a yellow one.

Many people are afraid of heights and yet heights can't hurt you (unless you suffer from altitude sickness) – not even the tiniest bit. Falling **off** them can - and because we don't trust ourselves **not** to fall, we see "heights" as terrifying. So is "height" the problem? Of course not – it's the perception of our **relationship** with heights that is the problem. You **have** to be prepared to look deeper with all of the issues that have held you back to date, and see if you can now see the **real** problem. Most times it will not be what you thought.

An important thought - is that the eyes actually don't see at all. The eyes are just collectors of light – it's the **mind** that turns the information brought in by our eyes, into images that we recognise or "see." So the eyes can be wide open as you just experienced, but if the mind is not, then we'll still - not see!

Fantastic - so we can start with a fully open mind **and** eyes then yes?

Go back to your **Draft Action Plan** and make a statement regarding what you are going to do, to ensure **your** mind remains open from here on.

Let's create a list aimed at what keeps people from living the life they want. Remember that "THINKING" is the central point, but let's work out from there. Check all of the following that apply to you...

~ Fear

~ Mistakes

~ Failure

~ Won't measure up

28

- ~ People won't like me
- ~ Lose everything
- ~ Being hurt
- ~ Don't know what I want out of life/can have out of life
- ~ Lack of enthusiasm
- ~ No direction
- ~ Attitude
- ~ Lack skills
- ~ Negative patterns/habits
- ~ No one to turn to
- ~ No money
- ~ Lack education
- ~ Overwhelmed by problems
- ~ Not a forgiving person
- ~ Low self-esteem
- ~ People will take advantage of me
- ~ Life in control of me
- ~ Worry a lot
- ~ Separation from "who you are"
- ~ Don't belong
- ~ Lonely
- ~ Ego
- ~ Guilt
- ~ Can't let go
- ~ Jealousy
- ~ Can't handle conflict
- ~ Can't relax
- ~ Struggle with relationships

- Add any that may not be on the list, but which you believe are standing in **your** way.

Colour in or mark in any way you want, the things that stand most firmly in the way of **your** living the life you want. This will become part of your "**Things To Work On**" page as we continue through the program.

Measurement

At the end of most if not all chapters will be an exercise. These exercises are intended to help you measure your learning and/or progress, and are **critically** important to the success of the program. When you can point to your own 'measurable achievements,' the whole program will have more meaning for you.

For many of you, the ego will already have jumped in and said "But you can't measure **everything**" and I disagree (as usual). I have not found anything yet that cannot be measured by one, or a combination, of the following:

1. Quality
2. Quantity
3. Time, and
4. Cost

As an example, someone once said to me "But you can't measure kindness" - and (of course) you **can**...

As an **un**kind person (for example), you will find that people avoid you (measurable? - you bet), you won't have many people that you can really call a friend (measurable? – uhuh), when you want to celebrate, people will have an amazing variety of reasons why they can't join you (measurable? – oh yeah), you probably don't get invited out a lot, and there's probably not a lot of joy in your life.

As you change your behaviour, so will you change people's perceptions of you. You will find more people wanting to spend time with you, and some may even start asking to include you in **their** activities.

So you **can** measure kindness - against Quantity – the number of people in your life, and Quality – the amount of enjoyment in your life. Take it from there

Suggestion
To get the absolute maximum out of this program - get some friends or your family to buy the book (or buy books for them as a gift), and treat it as a workshop.

Get together once a week or whatever works for you, maybe get a different person to read each chapter to the group aloud, and agree to keep one another on track. This will lift your chances of gaining the best from the program tremendously.

However you approach this – please don't treat it as a crash course and try to do it in two days. I absolutely recommend that you do a **maximum** of a chapter at a time – once a week. Write down **all** the things that were most relevant to you (or that impacted you the most as you read) and alongside of them – write what you're going to **do** about it.

Then at your next session – take a look at what you **said** you were going to do and compare it to what you actually **did**. If you have found excuses for not having done anything then I recommend that you wait until you **have** done them, before moving on.

Exercise:
1. Go through all of the things that I asked you to do in this chapter, and ensure that you agree with what you've done so far.

2. Ensure that you have listed everything that you feel has stood in your way in the past, what might continue to do that, and what you are going to do about it in your **Personal Discoveries** & **Draft Action Plan** pages, and

3. Print and fill out the **Getting The Most** questionnaire before proceeding.

Chapter 3

EGO

No one has ever seen the face of ego. It is like a ghost that we accept as a controlling influence in our lives. The reason no one has seen the ego is because the ego is only a thought. - Tagore

Introduction

This is a tough chapter to write because in order to understand the ego and its place in our lives, you almost **have** to include the "spiritual" part of our "being." This is **not** intended to be a lesson in spirituality, and nor is it intended to interfere with any person's concept of religion; so please don't let your ego turn it into that, and cause you to miss the most important part of your opportunity to transform your life. The ego absolutely **detests** hearing about itself and will come up with a million reasons as to why you should avoid this section.

> The ego is the root of **all** that is negative in our lives.
>
> *Tom Grbich*

Read this chapter as many times as you need to – but **don't move on until you fully understand it.** *The ego is at the root of **all** that is negative in our lives. Tom Grbich.*

The ultimate block to everything we are about to do - to our hopes and dreams, to learning, to having healthy relationships (with ourselves let alone with others), and to living the life we want is indisputably – the ego!

Warning: This is 'spooky' but you just watch it happen – this (for many of you) will be the hardest part of the book to read and/or grasp. These are some of the words you will very likely "hear" in your mind as you move on….

"This is boring, what a load of crap, what's the point, don't you have something better to do, - actually, I really should get that grass mowed before it rains… blah, blah, blah." (Typical ego talk).

If for any reason you don't finish the manual, for your own sake -

please don't stop until you have read **and understood** this section at least. I guarantee you that if you are not living the life that you **want** to live, the ego will be the major player by far, in ensuring that you never do.

Objective

By the end of this chapter you will be able to describe...

~ What the ego is

~ Why it exists

~ How to begin taking your "life" back

~ How it will fight you, and

~ How to deal with it

What is the ego?

The ego is an illusion – it is nothing more than the perception you have of your "self." Ego as a "thing" doesn't exist - it is a (dangerous) illusion that feeds on and promotes your weaknesses. If you continue to give it power, you are unlikely **ever** to discover who or what you really are, or what your potential really is.

Unfortunately, it is not something that you can ever be totally without because in a sense, the ego is the part of us that allows us to participate in this consciousness. So we simply **have** to learn to deal with it.

When we are born, we tend to forget where we came from, and we see this "life" as the "reality," even while knowing that it's just a blink in the eye of eternity.

Insane

Many of us have allowed the ego to become so powerful that it controls every aspect of our lives - an incredibly dangerous situation when you consider that the ego is **totally and completely – insane.**

~ It will convince you that you can't do things that you absolutely, categorically **can.**

~ It will tell you that other people "can't stand you" when in fact they may adore you, or have no opinion of you at all - either way.

~ It will tell you people adore you when they actually can't stand you.

~ It will convince you that no one could **ever** love you, when people are lining up to be with you

~ It will find ways to trash all of your achievements so that you don't appreciate them

~ It will cause you to end "perfect" relationships because of a single "wrong", and

~ It will convince you that **you** are "different" or your **situation** is "different," even though the proof is all around you - that that is not true.

Freeing yourself from the illusions of the ego will be easier when you recognise its characteristics and how it works.

Tagore touches on the falsity of the ego in this enlightened statement:

"He whom I enclose with my name is weeping in this dungeon. I am ever busy building this wall all around; and as this wall goes up into the sky day by day I lose sight of my true being in its dark shadow. I take pride in this great wall, and I plaster it with dust and sand lest a least hole should be left in this name; and for all the care I take, I lose sight of my true being."

The wall is the ego that **we** empower - imprisoning us in a dungeon of frustration.

When we begin to entertain the concept that we are a body with a soul (as opposed to a soul with a body), we enter a world of confusion.

~ We make assumptions about what will make us happy, and we end up frustrated

~ We push to promote our self-importance as we yearn for a deeper and richer life experience

~ We fill our lives with "expectations," and wonder why we are continually disappointed

~ We make assumptions about what will make us happy, and we end up frustrated

~ We push to promote our self-importance as we yearn for a deeper and richer life experience

~ We fill our lives with "expectations," and wonder why we are continually disappointed, and

~ We fall into the void of self-absorption repeatedly; not knowing that the surest escape is merely to discard the false idea of who we are.

A fully empowered ego is incredible to see – it can convince you that you are fat when you look like a skeleton; it can convince you that you have all the skill of a boiled potato, when you in fact may be the best in the field. I had a lady in my martial art class who was as good as anyone I had ever taught but she ultimately left, because she could not be persuaded that she wasn't holding the class back.

The ego is all about self obsession – it's **all** about you – everything! You can have a life of ease – a fabulous partner, a wonderful home in a nice area, nice things, no financial concerns, and still be a mire of self pity and depression, willing to lose everything you have (including your partner), rather than wake up and put the ego to rest.

Logic
The ego is an absolute master of "logic" – especially when it comes to justifying your actions, and even how you feel sometimes. Logically, is it 'wrong' to expect someone to say "Thank you" for a favour done?

If you help someone in need, is it 'wrong'" to expect that they will help you in **your** time of need? Of course "logically" the answer must be "No – it **isn't** wrong" in either case. But the thing that most often follows expectation is disappointment and why would you grant someone the power to disappoint you (if you don't like disappointment)? Do things for others that you **want** to do, and let your reward be the satisfaction that comes from doing it, rather than the expectation that you will get a return. There always **is** a return, but sometimes it will come from someone or something far removed from the original act on your part.

Separation

The ego is **committed** to having you believe the illusion of separateness. With each painful experience of feeling alone, apart or separate, like a python - the ego tightens its hold. The most effective way it can do this is to convince us that our low self-esteem is totally justified.

The most natural thing in the world is to imagine that others see us as **we** do, and if it's obvious that someone does **not** see us that way, the ego convinces us that they're only being "nice" to us - because they "feel sorry for us." It's "charity."

Thought:
An extremely interesting exercise is to take a shoebox for example, cut a bunch of holes in the lid - some big, some small, and some in between. Then cut a hole in one end and attach a viewer that allows you to look through the hole without letting in any additional light.
If you took the box outside into the sunlight and looked through the viewer - what do you think you would see?

Yes there would be all these wonderful shafts of light - some looking big and important, some small and insignificant, and some maybe even brighter than others. Just like people huh?

And that's the way it would always be until we removed the lid - and discovered there was actually only **one** light. Isn't it incredibly sad that **by far** the greater part of the world's population will die, without **ever** taking the lid off?

Convinced of our separateness, we view life as a competitive exercise - our concern is that there are **so many** others who are "better" than we are. Unable to accept that like the shafts of light in the shoebox - we are all "one," our anxiety mounts, and our sense of aloneness drives us to seek our connectedness, happiness, etc - outside.

> By **far** the greatest part of the world's population will die without ever taking the lid off.
>
> *Tom Grbich*

Your need to look better, achieve more, accumulate more, judge others and find fault, are all symptoms of the erroneous belief that you are disconnected and separate.

This idea of separateness begins early in life after all – we **are** a body with a soul (remember) and we can **see** that our body is separate from the other bodies (just like lights in the shoe-box right?).

Without someone to model a more holistic life on, we grow up experiencing the pain of loneliness, injuries and peer criticism, all of which intensifies feelings of being apart from, rather than a part **of**, whatever it is that the universe is made up of.

We become convinced that the physical life is all there is; we spend a lot of time comparing - believing we are better than others (or they are better than we are); and our interpersonal philosophy becomes one of "getting the best of the other guy first" or they'll certainly do it to you. Lack of purpose and meaning in life is confirmed by the belief that you are born, you shop, you suffer and you die.

Since this ego illusion is all there is to life, it becomes important to fight for what we want, and to hoard – the classic "scarcity versus abundance" concept.

The price of ego
Your ego **works** for its living. Its payoff is in keeping its power over you which it does by nurturing a rather smooth-flowing river of misery, filled with fears about your inadequacy and shortcomings.

Your ego is in direct conflict with your true purpose in this life which is to learn, have fun, and to give (and receive) love.

Guilt
Your ego absolutely **thrives** on guilt – often coming from the "mistakes" that we see ourselves making - and yet the reality is that mistakes are where our greatest learning comes from.

> You are here to **learn**, have **fun**, and to give (and receive) love.
>
> *Tom Grbich*

Guilt is the inner belief that you should pay
a price for every mistake you have ever made in your life.

Love
Your ego doesn't reject love – heck, love provides so **many** opportunities for misery after all. It merely provides you with excuses

as to why you should be skeptical - that people extending their love to you probably "want something," and that you are sure to be taken advantage of, if you give your love too freely to others.

Appearing to be acting in your very best interests, the ego wisely advises that love is a high ideal, but one that is loaded with danger - there is a good chance you'll get hurt, so you should proceed 'cautiously.' It warns you to "limit the amount of love you give because you may be taken advantage of." People will always be trying to take advantage of you, because that's what this world is all about.

All of those ideas keep you in a state of fear, not panic, just fear. A consistent anxiety about giving and receiving love is enough to keep you firmly under the influence of ego for life.

Ego promotes **false** love. In your relationships with others, your ego convinces you that your partner is "just what you need," to fill the emptiness inside you. Any relationship arising from this belief will never embrace **true** love and peace because it makes you a dependant.

By definition, if you are incomplete, that's all you will have to give away, because you can't give away what you don't possess. You will give your partner an incomplete person who is afraid of being discovered! There is no way that authentic love can flourish in such a dishonest atmosphere. You will be unable to truly experience love or to receive it, without questioning it.

The end result?
The end result of this "separate" belief for many; is loneliness — crushing, debilitating loneliness.

Put ego in its rightful place
When ego has been put in its rightful place you'll no longer need to compete or be "better" than anyone. There'll be no need to accumulate, achieve, or seek outer honours for any reason other than for your own satisfaction. You will have left behind an idea that you may have cultivated for most of your life.

Rather than view yourself as **distinct** from your perception of "God" (and everyone else), you'll experience your life as **connected** to them - free from separation.

You'll experience a connectedness to your 'self' and all of life, in a way that ego's illusion couldn't begin to comprehend. And you'll never truly feel lonely again.

I left my first marriage in February 1988 – one of the toughest decisions I ever made, and one by one, all of my friends quickly "disappeared."

As Christmas neared, one of the guys in my martial art class asked what I was doing for Christmas, and I explained that I hadn't decided. I **had** decided not to go north and visit my Mum that year, but didn't know what I would do in place of that.

He then offered to have me spend Christmas day with him and his parents, and a decision presented itself... I told him I felt Christmas was for family and I wasn't family, so perhaps I would come in the evening. I would spend Christmas day in the bush – one of my favourite places to be, and the place where I felt most "connected." Part way through one of the gorges on the way to my Mum's place – (about an hour's drive from Auckland), was a little one-lane gravel road that just "disappeared" off the main road, and into the native bush. Every time I had passed that road over the years, I had thought to myself that "One day I will investigate where that goes."

So Christmas day arrived – a beautiful sunny day without a breath of wind, and I set off to spend some time with myself. I went into the bush and spent perhaps the loneliest day since childhood there, with no idea of why I was there, or where I would go from there. As dusk began to fall I headed back towards the car and a flash of anger raced through me. I thought "This is crazy – I've lost my friends, I've lost my wife and my home, I've never had a family to speak of, and I don't even have a country that I can call home" (while I was raised in New Zealand – it never felt like my "home"). The thought continued, "I don't belong **anywhere**" and at that instant, the first breeze of the day swept through the trees bringing the thought with it, "No you don't belong anywhere. You are a child of the universe and wherever you are – is where you belong." It was an unbelievably profound instant in time for me, and I have never felt lonely since.

Taking your life back

How do you start taking control back? Firstly, you need to learn how to recognise when your **ego** is in control, as opposed to your **"heart"** (your "reality" centre).

It's unbelievably important to separate the word **can't** – from **won't**. For example "I just can't **possibly** get up and speak to a group of people that I don't know." **Millions** of people will relate to that one - and what a load of hippo muck **that** is! All you have to do is stand up, walk to the podium, stand in front of the microphone, open your mouth and make words.

Of **course** you **can** do that – but you **won't** – because you're "too shy," because you "might not be able to think of anything to say," because "people might laugh at you"... because, because, because... see how the excuses fly when the ego has control?

Whenever you hear the word "can't" from here on, you absolutely **know** that your ego is in charge, and you simply **have** to change that. The most damaging lie of all - is the one that you tell to yourself.

Be **honest** with yourself – there is very little in this world that you **really** can't do or can't **learn** to do, so get that excuse out of your life. I'm not saying that you will be **good** at doing everything, but don't say you "can't" do it because that is the greatest limiter of all. It is nothing but a pathetic cop-out and there's no other way to put it!

The good news is that taking control of your ego is **REALLY, REALLY** simple, (although the ego will do all in its power to convince you otherwise of course).

Just ask the question "How do I **FEEL** right now?" The more regularly you check in and (more importantly) **DO** something about it - the sooner you'll be free of the crippling effects of ego. When you ask that question - what are you looking for? Read on...

Two states
There are only two states in reality and they are "**Ok**" or "**NOT Ok**." An "Ok" state will involve words like "peace, tranquility, joy, happiness, love, hope, humility, kindness, generosity, truth," etc. **Any**

other state suggests the presence of ego.

A "Not Ok" state will involve words like "Fear, Guilt, Jealousy, Anger, Hurt, loneliness, envy, regret, greed, inferiority, depression," etc.

Appreciate that depression in particular, **can** be due to hormonal and/or chemical reasons so don't assume that **all** of your issues are ego based – check it out.

In most instances by far however, the "not ok" state is ego driven, and the "ok" state is the absence of ego. Where this is **never** true of course, is when you are in genuine danger – if you are in the middle of the African jungle and you hear the crashing of a large beast heading in your direction – I promise you it is not ego if you suddenly feel "not ok" about that!

Think about it - your soul / spiritual being, or whatever else you like to call it has no need **whatsoever**, to feel fear, anger, hatred, self-consciousness, greed, etc. It is **eternal** and indestructible, so why would it need to concern itself with garbage like that? Experiencing those feelings where there is no justification highlights the separation between you and your soul.

Food for thought
Considering that the "Ok" states are generally associated with "positives" - a state that does **not** seem to fit is "sadness." Sadness is mostly looked upon as a negative feeling but personally, I don't see it that way.

Grief I do regard as a negative emotion because it suggests "loss" (of something that you never owned anyway), and attachment. While grief and sadness are often used together, I believe that although there **may** be times when sadness is an ego state, I personally believe that genuine sadness is more often a true "state of the heart."

How it will fight you
When the ego catches on to the fact that you are working to take your life back – **expect trouble!**

It will be an excuse-a-minute scenario where you will be able to come up with every reason in the universe as to why you should dump this program, burn the book, leave the country, and forget everything you have learned here. The ego **never** gives up – **ever**.

Learn to love the ego

Face it - you cannot get rid of the ego and anyone who says they don't have one, has an ego sitting up there saying "yesss" because it **knows** it has him/her totally in its grip. The only way to limit the ego to the role for which it was created, is to **love** it. It is an extremely clever and cunning "child" that will never give up trying to win back its control – for as long as you are alive.

> The ego **never** gives up – **ever**!
>
> *Tom Grbich*

Sometimes it helps to consider how you would **deal** with such a child. You could call the child over (having caught it doing something wrong) – scream at it, smash it, think of a more terrifying way of punishing it or, you could call him over – give him ten points for ingenuity in his attempt to get around a rule, remind him that this new action **still** contravenes that rule, and send him away after a big hug. I know which path **I** prefer to take, and I hope you think that way too.

Remember that the ego is the conscious part of "you" so when you find yourself raging having caught it in action again – you are raging at **yourself** - and feeding ice cream and pie to the ego in the process. It just doesn't make sense! The greatest of all learning comes from dealing with obstacles, and nothing in our world can come up with more obstacles than the ego. So love it for the lessons it brings you, **but don't give it your power**.

In summary

Your ego is the part of your **own** mind, which exists so that you can be here – the conscious mind deals with - the consciousness.

You can begin taking your life back by getting real – dealing with, and from, your heart instead of being in your head all the time. This in no way suggests that you should give "thought" away. Remember that the conscious mind understands the conscious**ness** better than the heart does, but thought should always be tempered by what is felt in the heart.

42

Your ego will try to prevent that by attempting to convince you that everything about what you are planning to do is wrong, stupid, crazy, and so on. It will find a dozen reasons a minute as to why you should not continue with this manual for example, but if you really think about them – **none** of those reasons will (really) make sense.

You will know when your **ego** is in control when:

~ You are constantly **"beating yourself up"** for perceived "mistakes" or "errors of judgment"

~ You are generally unhappy/depressed

~ There is always someone or something to '**blame'** for all that is "wrong" in your life

~ You spend a lot of time in a state of **anxiety and fear**

~ There are lots of things that really **"piss you off"** about life in general, or about the people around you

~ You find yourself **judging** others (and yourself) a lot

~ You are forever helping others to **"sort their lives out"** when your own is in a mess

~ You find yourself pulling others **down** rather than lifting yourself **up**

~ You feel "**alone**" a lot - sometimes even in a crowd

~ There is always a "good reason" for feeling the way you do

~ It's important for you to be "right" all the time

~ You're afraid to give unconditional love

~ People are saying nice things about you but you just can't accept their truth

~ You **need others** around you, in order to be "happy," and

~ You are forever searching for answers "**out there**" - looking for books or people, who can "enlighten" you

You'll know when **you** are in control when...

~ You can see your mistakes as the most **natural school of learning,** and accept that you'll **continue** to make them until you have wings on your back

- You have almost **forgotten** what fear and anxiety feel like
- **Nothing** "pisses you off" any longer (unless you consciously choose to let it)
- You find yourself **accepting** others rather than **judging** them
- You **act** responsibly towards other people but don't try to **take** responsibility for them
- You don't 'blame' any longer – you take full responsibility for both the 'good' **and** the 'bad' in your life
- You want to lift yourself **up,** and lift as many others up with you as possible
- You don't **care** who's right any longer – you're having way too much fun being **happy**
- You **never** feel alone - even when you are
- Happiness is something you **take with you** rather than **look for**
- You "**know**" the **real** answers are all inside you, and
- The bigger the battle put up by your ego - the closer you are to neutering it, by taking back your power.

The most important rule for getting to the "Ok" state more than 90% of the time is to **continually, regularly check in** with - "How am I **feeling** right now" or "How do I **feel** about this?" Remember that any feeling that is not aligned with happiness, peace, joy, tranquility, justness, etc is the best indication you'll have, that you are in ego.

And now it's up to you:

- Will you stay where you are - remembering that if you continue to do what you've always done, you'll continue to get what you've always got (at best – in **reality,** the world may just move on without you)
- Will you lift the lid occasionally and just dream about what might be, or will you
- Blow the whole damned roof off and go claim everything that that wonderful life **is** holding in store for you out there, right now?

Exercise:

1. Note in your **Personal Discoveries** page where you believe your ego has held its greatest power over you in the past.

2. In your **Draft Action Plan**, note how you plan to take control back.

Print and read **Wolves**. Read it a hundred times!

Chapter 4

WHAT IT IS TO BE HUMAN

The purpose of this chapter is simply to help you appreciate that you're "not alone" in experiencing things that the current "fashion" says are "negative," and to get you to write down how **you** view **your** life, to date.

In one of my many roles I worked in a division of a large company that had the most toxic environment I have ever seen. My office became an oasis with a steady stream of people coming in throughout the day "just to share my space" as they put it.

On one occasion a gorgeous young lady (let's call her Jackie) came in. As she walked through the door she said "Oh Tom, I know you're not supposed to feel negative like this but this place has really p....d me off so don't let me interrupt you – I just need to share your space for a while."

I said "No problem," and as she sat on the couch, I walked around to the side and squashed my nose up against the glass wall. She looked at me for a moment then burst out laughing saying, "You idiot – what are you doing?"

I said, "I'm just trying to see what world **you** live in because it's obviously different to mine." She asked what I was talking about and I explained, "There is absolutely nothing **wrong** with feeling negative Jackie – you're human. **Staying** negative is a whole different issue and you're not doing that – you've come in here to get rid of those feelings and then you're going right back out there yes?" She agreed.

I then said, "When I look out there – I see the most toxic environment I have ever worked in but the difference is – I leave it out there – you've taken it on board" (an act of the ego of course). Unfortunately, the "positive thinking brigade" has just created another problem for people who now believe that if you feel negative – there's something wrong with you.

There **isn't** - you're just human and without the appropriate tools, the "negatives" of life **will** creep in from time to time. One of the major objectives of this manual is to give you the tools to keep those negatives **outside**, as I do.

Later in the program (when you have more "understanding" and the tools to work with), we'll come back and apply some of what we've learned, to changing the balances here.

By the end of this chapter you'll be able to identify in your own words:

~ Where **your** high/low self esteem originates

~ What causes your up times / down times

~ The environments leading to the times we cope Vs the times we don't

~ The average time you spend in joy - in impotent rage or anger, or in just plain misery - where it comes from, how you feel about that, and where you want the averages to change

~ Why it is that there are times we want company / times we don't

~ What obligations/challenges you individually relish Vs those you resent, even fear. What is the difference, and what you can personally do about it, and

~ How to deal with confrontation.

It's interesting to consider why so many people do struggle with their self-esteem, some, a lot, some all the time. Thinking back to what you have learned so far - why do you think that is? Yes... it's because they have been **taught** to feel that way, by parents, peers, environment, and so on.

Of course the ego just **loves** that – maintaining low self-esteem is almost **entirely** an ego thing. If you suffer from low self esteem at any time – consider where that is coming from (what information are you basing that on)? In other words... what is the ego using to make you feel that way? Write your thoughts in your **Personal Discoveries Page** along with the items below.

When you allow yourself to discover who you **really** are, you will very likely be amazed.

Up times - down times – what causes **your** up times? Write them down and if you are working with a group – explore any or all of these things with them. What causes your down times? Again – make a list.

Times we cope - times we don't. Do you ever feel at times that you just aren't coping? When do you find yourself coping the best? When typically, do you find yourself struggling? What have you done to change that in the past? Write it all down.

Sometimes in joy - sometimes in impotent rage/anger/frustration, other times just plain miserable. Write down the amount of your waking hours (on average) that you currently spend in joy (you must be honest about this). How do you feel about that? What would you like to change here?

Times we want company - times we don't. When do you find yourself wanting company? What is going on inside you at those times where you just want to be left alone? Is it really a problem (wanting to be alone)? If so – why, and what can be done about it?

Obligations/challenges we relish - others we resent - even fear. What is it about those obligations or challenges that you relish? What about the ones that you resent or fear? What's the difference, and what do you think you can you do about this? Write it down.

I'm going to take you through an exercise now that I think you will find pretty enlightening - even amazing. I want you to imagine that I am offering you a sum of money for the various parts of your body (let's assume that I am going to donate them to other people with medical problems). It's important that you are totally "real" about this – in other words – I am going to actually remove the parts listed. So how much money would you really want, before you were willing to give me...?

The fingers of your right hand $_____

The fingers of your left hand $_____

Your right hand $_____

Your left hand $_____

Your right arm $_____

Your left arm	$_____
Your right eye	$_____
Your left eye	$_____
Your hearing	$_____
Your right foot	$_____
Your left foot	$_____
Your whole right leg	$_____
Your whole left leg	$_____
Now add up the total	$_____

Please go to your **Personal Discoveries Page** now and write down in big, bold letters – I now see my **own** value as a person, as being **MORE** than (whatever your total sum came to. The reason we put "more than" is because we didn't look at lungs, kidneys etc that can also be removed without killing you.

Now if you had a car or a home worth just a million dollars and it was the only one you were ever going to have – how well would you look after it? My hope is that you saw yourself being worth **way** more than that – so what do you think would happen if you treated yourself with (at least) the same amount of respect, and looked after yourself as well as you are telling me that you would look after that home or car?

Put that statement somewhere where you will see it every day, and answer the question – "When would you like to start (taking care of **yourself** that well)?" And what will that look like (what specifically, are you going to **do** to pamper yourself on a daily basis)?

It's important to understand that the only reason I asked you to see yourself in monetary terms is because we tend to understand the **value** of money more than anything else.

You probably know that (at the time of writing this) Bill Gates is one of the wealthiest men in the world – consider whether or not you would accept Bill's wealth if you knew the instant the deal was closed, you would become an immediate paraplegic and within one month, you would have advanced Alzheimer's disease?

As much as you may or may not like the body you were given – how much do you think someone like Bill Gates would be prepared to **pay** for that body in place of his/her own, if he knew he was about to get terminal cancer, or that hideous flesh eating disease (Ebola)?

What have you learned from this exercise? Hopefully, you will have a whole new view of your worth, and the importance of your health.
Taking better care of "you" begins, with taking better care of your (overall) health. In essence, there are four things necessary for you to enjoy the best possible health in this lifetime. They are:

~   Healthy thinking

~   A healthy spine

~   A healthy intake (clean air, clean water, and good nutrition), and

~   Rest

We'll look at this more closely in a later section but consider that if the mind controls the whole of the body and your thinking is unhealthy, then it stands to reason that your body will soon follow suit. Stress is now accepted as the number one cause of cancer in women – worldwide. Think about that – what does stress do? It "consumes" your every waking minute - and eventually, your body follows suit – consuming **itself** with cancer.   Whatever is in your mind, will ultimately show in your body.

A healthy spine – the nerves are the two-way communication channel between the brain and the body, and almost **all** of the nerves of the body pass through the spinal column, via the spinal cord.

If the spine is subluxated then all kinds of erroneous signals are going to go back and forth (or not), and your health will certainly suffer. See a good chiropractor (if you can find one), and get treatments at least once every three months or as needed. Especially though – learn the exercises that support and maintain the spine, and then chiropractors will be less of a necessity.

A healthy intake – even the best engines in the world do not run well on poor fuel so why would you expect your body to? Clean air, water, and nutrition are sometimes hard to come by but we should do our best at all times. Avoid smokers, car fumes, and stagnant air as much as possible, purchase a good water filter; buy organic foods where possible, and diligently wash vegetables and fruits. Although GMF is purported to be totally safe – how do we know? They haven't been around long enough and while genetic modification has been taking place since the beginning of time, it has **never** occurred across species before (ever tried mating a frog with a tomato?)

In particular though – check the labels on everything you buy. You won't **believe** how much crap is in there that doesn't need to be. In Canada my children compared a block of cheese with New Zealand cheese, and found that there was nearly double the number of ingredients in the Canadian cheese. Why?

When I found that Canadian bread may have as many as 60 (unlisted) chemicals in it, I bought a bread-maker immediately, and I bake all our own bread now.

Rest – this is often abused even more than the others. No matter **how** tough you think you are – the body just cannot function without rest. We don't all need the same **amount** of rest, but we all do need **some**. Listen to your body and obey its needs, and everything about your life will be better.

Exercise:
Go to your **Draft Action Plan** and describe what you are going to do to take better care of those areas of your life from now on.

Chapter 5

LOOKING AT YOURSELF
The purpose of this chapter is to get you to look at some of the things that have **led** you to the things (good or bad) that life has dealt to you (again I'd like you to write these down in your "**Personal Discoveries**" page). Most of these things we'll deal with right away, but we **will** come back where appropriate.

By the end of this chapter you will be able to:
~ List the patterns of your lifetime, categorising them as positive or negative

~ List what you want to change and why

~ List people you'll model your changes on

~ Discuss how you can start being who you really want to be

~ Discuss the ultimate forgiveness - forgiving yourself, and

~ Identify how you can begin loving (and learning from) your "mistakes"

Patterns of a lifetime - the good and the bad
So - what sorts of things do you think I'm talking about with regard to "patterns?"

Patterns are the conditioning of the past - they're the basis of our habits - and many times, they become our personal prisons.

When you take a creature that was born to be free and place it in a confined space, it will explore every inch or centimetre of its cage – looking for a way out. Often it will try to break free - risking injury in the process, and some will even pine away and die. Eventually though, most will come to accept their restriction, and often the **final** effect, is where they come to feel **comfortable** with that restriction. They begin to accept that this is all their world will ever be.

The same thing happens to people and like people, there will always be those ones who will never stop looking for a way out, as long as they are alive. There will also be those that fade away and die without their freedom and interestingly, freedom is the "need" that people are most **willing** to die for.

The frightening thing is that when that "acceptance" has taken place, the creature will often remain as **though** imprisoned even after the confining cage is removed. Fleas are trained to jump to a certain height by placing glass panels at the desired height. Groups of fleas jump – bang their heads, jump - bang their heads again, and after a bunch of migraines they finally learn how high they can jump, and **not** bang their heads. Then, even when the panel is removed, that's as high as they will jump forever after.

Wild elephants in Borneo are trained similarly. They have steel bands with chains placed around their feet and they soon learn that you can **try** to escape, but all that happens is that it hurts, and you don't go anywhere – no matter **how** hard you try. Once that conditioning has been implanted in their minds, all that is required to restrain them from then on, is pressure around their leg. A small rope that they could break in a blink, will bind them as securely as the real thing.

Reviewing the comment above about animals that have been placed in a cage until they become comfortable with their new environment; it's extremely interesting to learn that when you finally take the cage **down**, they will often become **extremely** distressed and fearful, and sometimes will even attack you to try to **stop** you from freeing them. (Of course there will always be the rare ones though, that will just run as fast as they can and never look back).

Many of us have been in our own **virtual prisons** for most of our lives - confined by our beliefs right or wrong, and often we too become frightened when someone starts to dismantle the prison walls from around us. As we begin bringing your awareness to **your** personal prisons/patterns, don't be surprised if you find a part of **yourself** feeling frightened, and fighting to "protect" them too. (And we know which part that will be don't we?)

Take some time to write down your "patterns" as you see them (in your **Personal Discoveries page**/s) and put them in two columns - positive and negative. When you've done that, put an asterisk beside those that you'd especially like to change, and if you **really** want to get a jump-start to achieving the life you'd like to live, then list them in order of priority.

Print and read "**The Black Door**"

Often, a good way of getting yourself heading in the right direction to being the person you want to be, and living the life you want to live, is to consider other people whom you've encountered in your life as a model. They may have been people in a movie or story, a friend, or even a fictional character in a book. Ask what qualities drew you to them, that you'd maybe like to adopt. Make a note of anyone you can think of, and the qualities you want to emulate.

One thing that has always amazed me as an adult, is that even in the worst times of my life as a child - in my dreams I was always Superman - out saving the world.

What do you think you're going to need to do in order to start making those changes? Write down these thoughts, and put asterisks or whatever beside those things where you just don't know where to start.

One of the things that you will hear over and over is that in order to be able to get rid of the past – you have to learn to forgive

I DISAGREE!

In order to forgive, you first have to **judge** that someone has done something wrong. This path will take you into "blame," with blame comes the absolving of responsibility (it's now Mum's fault, society's fault... blah blah blah), and it's all downhill from there. So perhaps the first thing that needs to be looked at is "who are we to judge" and "was/is that judgement appropriate?" If you can accept that everything happens for a reason, then look for the learning – not the "judgement," that supposedly needs "forgiving."

So, forgive **yourself** if you must, but don't pull yourself down by the need to "forgive" others. And be very sure of what you are forgiving yourself **for** – is it for being **human**?

> Until you have wings on your back – **you will continue to screw up from time to time.**
>
> *Tom Grbich*

And isn't that what we're supposed to be?

Until you have wings on your back you will continue to screw up from time to time so get over it – it's not only okay – it's the way it's supposed to be!

Seriously, the things that we punish ourselves (sometimes to **death**) for is amazing. And what part of you just drools at the thought of you making yourself feel guilty? Yes of course – our friend the ego!

At one time in my first marriage, my wife and I applied for an AFS student (a student from overseas who comes to live with you as a part of your family for a year). As the girl came out from the passenger area of the airport, I couldn't help notice the vivid rashes on the inner elbows of both arms, and one extending from her ear down to the top of her shoulder.

The fact that she was making no attempt to hide them indicated that she was not bothered by them, which was good. I waited until she had had time to settle in before asking her how long she'd had them, and what she was doing about them.

She told me she had had them for as long as she could remember, and her Mum had spent thousands on treatments, but nothing seemed to work. Appreciating that some skin complaints are psychosomatic, I asked if she would like to find out if it was something in her past, or whether it was a medical condition that she had. She was very keen to get to the bottom of it and although the fact that she could not remember anything about her father who died when she was nine bothered me, with her Mum's permission, I used hypnosis to see what I could find.

To cut a long story short, we found that she had been punishing herself since her father died because she did not go to the funeral, and "how could he know that she loved him when she didn't even go to say goodbye?" She was nine years old at the time.

Soon after dealing with that, (forgiving herself?) the rashes disappeared and to the best of my knowledge – they never came back.

Question – have you ever made a mistake in your lifetime? You've made **lots** of them?

Congratulations!!!
Can you honestly say that you **like** making mistakes?

No? Actually – neither do I but...

Here is a little exercise that I want you to do every time you feel guilty about having screwed up **again**...

1. Stand up

2. Place one hand over your shoulder and...

3. Feel around as far down your back as you can

I'm **serious** about this – it's time to laugh at yourself for a change, instead of beating yourself up.

Now when you did that – did you find any wings? **No**? What can that possibly mean?

I'll **tell** you what it means – it means that you are still **alive**, you're **human**, and that means it is your **responsibility** to go and make **more** mistakes, because that is the source of the greatest of life's lessons!

Think about it – if you decided that you wanted to learn to sail and I took you out every weekend for two years, but we only went out if the wind was below 8 knots and the sun was shining - what would you have learned about sailing at the end of that time – **really**? If I then took you out one night in a storm – **that's** when you'd find out what you knew about sailing!

The reality is – you don't learn a darned thing when you're cruising, so start learning to **appreciate** your mistakes and use them as a measure, of how much you have learned. As your mistakes become fewer and fewer, and further and further apart – you have your own measure of the fact that you are improving.

> The greatest mistake a person can make, is to be afraid of making one.
>
> *Originator unknown*

The greatest mistake that a person can make; is to be afraid of making one.

Now I know this "loving your mistakes" stuff may sound a bit idealistic or a bit wishy washy to some of you, so I'm going to tell you about something that happened to me, and **you** judge whether it was a "mistake" or not.

In one of my sales roles, I had been in the job only about a month when I got an appointment with one of the General Managers of one of New Zealand's largest companies, to demonstrate our personality profiling system. No one in the company had been able to achieve this in more than ten years. It was all the more exciting because he promised that if he liked what he saw, then he would help me introduce it to the other General Managers in the company.

I turned up for the appointment five minutes early, and went up to his reception where his Personal Assistant (PA) met me. She took my name, advised "Frank" that I was there, and then came back to take me to his office.

As I went through the door I was met with an **extremely** disgruntled - "You're late!"

Apologising as I checked my diary, I confirmed that I had 1pm as the appointment time, but somehow his schedule had my visit listed at 12pm. His attitude indicated that he was not at all impressed so, apologising for the mistake, I said, "Obviously I've messed up your schedule, so would you prefer that I organise to come back at another time?"

His response was "If you leave now – you won't be coming back."
So, promising to give him the best presentation I could while keeping it as short as possible, I sat down at the other side of his desk where, as I was getting my notes out – he announced that he needed a cup of coffee, and asked if I wanted one.

Under the concept of "When in Rome – do as the Romans do" I thanked him for the offer and agreed to join him.

His PA went away – returning shortly after with two cups of coffee, and I then proceeded to spill mine all over a presentation that he was working on getting out that afternoon.

So – can you see any mistakes there? Of course not – I don't make mistakes! (Yeah right)!

The rest of the meeting was as cold as a meat store and I got out of there as quickly as I could. Frank was the gruffest, most curt person I have ever encountered – before or since.

On the way back to work I considered what I could do to resurrect things - what would **you** have done?

On arriving back at work I was met with a **very** disappointed Manager. Apparently Frank had phoned to find out where I was, so everyone knew that I was (at least in Frank's mind) late for the appointment.

What I ultimately did was to write Frank a letter as follows... (word for word other than necessary changes to protect identities)

Dear Frank

Just a note to express my sincere appreciation for the time you gave to assessing our unique personality profiling system, and the assistance you so kindly offered to promoting the system within your company.

Having done with the formalities, I would also like to say how much pleasure it gave me to spill my coffee over your reports and of course I will expect similar opportunities to be offered on future visits to your office.

I would also like to point out that two whole days have passed since you ruined my image here at work by making it public that I had fouled up on the appointment, and I still haven't heard from the other Managers that you were lining up to contact me about our system.

I look forward to your explanation.
Kind regards
Etc.

So was **that** a mistake? My boss certainly thought so as he tried to intercept the posting of the letter but here is the response – received seven days later...

Dear Tom
Thank you for your brief epistle dated...

Firstly, let me say it was my pleasure to provide you with the occasion to discuss with me the elements of your integrated profiling system and to spray with gay abandon, desiccated cocoa beans all over my presentation to a manufacturer.

I fully expected to be swimming with the proposal as it was, but stap my vitals in coffee? Seriously though, it was my pleasure to be of what assistance it was.
Regards....

Now, would you **still** call it a mistake? If **my** thinking at the time had been that it was a mistake at any level, what do you think the result would have been? In my experience - a mistake only **remains** a mistake if you don't **learn** from it, and you'd be **amazed** at what you can **do** with your mistakes sometimes - all it takes is imagination.

> A mistake only **remains** a mistake if you don't **learn** from it.
>
> *Tom Grbich*

To complete the story – yes I **did** get business from them, and no I was not being frivolous in my response. On the way back I was trying to find a loophole, and it came in the belief that **somewhere** under that grumpy exterior was a sense of humour and if I could just tap into it somehow, I would have my resolution.

We ultimately became good friends and mutual mentors, and when I asked him what my chances of success would have been had I followed the traditional means for attempting to recover from such a litany of errors, he laughed at me and said I would never have got back in the door.

I also asked "Frank" what had taken place when he got my letter and read it. His response had been to immediately get on the phone to my General Manager and get me fired. He was re-reading the letter as he dialed and at the fifth digit he laughed. He said he thought "this guy has got guts" – no one else he had ever known would have tried something like that and I won his on-going respect as a result.

Another thing to think about is "what did I have to lose" (besides my job) – we were not doing business with his company anyway, and everyone had given up trying so...?

The other thing to consider is that I doubt we would have had the opportunity to develop such a relationship if I had **not** made that "mistake" so, take it from there. **I** think it was one of the better of my (many) "mistakes."

On another occasion I was coaching a young lady (let's call her "Helen") who had been struggling terribly with a new role. She soon became the top performer by far in her group, and her professionalism was at the extreme.

Coincidentally, I had given her group a talk on mistakes – changing the way you "see" mistakes. (Go back to the "Belief/Attitude Cycle)...

~   Our **Information** throughout our lives has been that mistakes are "bad."

~   Our **belief** therefore is that we should try as hard as possible not to make them, we should hide from them, conceal them from others, and so on.

~   Our **Attitude** to mistakes is that we "don't like them (even **fear** them)."

~   The **result** (or consequence) of making mistakes, has been that we have often been punished for doing so...

~   Confirming our **Information** (that mistakes are bad) and the cycle has been unbroken (until now).

Anyhow, the impact of the following "mistake" was such that Helen completely forgot her training of the previous day as she came into my office in tears saying, "Oh Tom – I just don't know what to do."
I asked her what had happened, and she explained that she had given a hand scrawled (you would hardly call it written) document to the group assistant, expecting it to be typed and faxed to her client. In the day-to-day rush however, the assistant had missed the "typing" part and faxed it as is.

I asked if she saw that as a mistake and to her, it was more than that – it was a **disaster**.

With questioning she remembered (her "new information") that mistakes were now to be seen as **opportunities**, and as coincidence would have it, our company had been running a series of major ads – telling people of the huge leaps in the quality of our service, and the **speed** especially, with which we now responded to our clients.

Bringing her thoughts to those ads, she finally saw the opportunity for some humour and my suggestion was that she call her client right away and ask if he had seen the ads (not the fax).   When he responded, she was to tell him that we had got **so** fast, that the document had bypassed the assistant and faxed itself before it could even be typed.   Somewhat dubious she asked, "Can I really **do** that?" "What else have you got," I asked?

Minutes later she was back in my office – **still** in tears but this time, with a huge smile on her face. She said her client just "cracked up." He laughed and laughed, saying that he had been wondering at the professionalism and that was the best excuse he'd heard in a long time.   The laughter broke down his resistance, and she got a sale where his decision otherwise might still have been in question.

> The greatest danger of fearing your mistakes, is that you won't take risks.
>
> *Tom Grbich*

One of the greatest dangers of **fearing** mistakes is that you won't take the risks that so often play a huge part in success; in case you "mess up" along the way.

Risks

To laugh is to risk appearing the fool;
To weep is to risk appearing sentimental
To reach out to another is to risk involvement
To expose your feelings, is to risk your true self
To place your ideas, your wishes, your dreams, before a crowd is to risk their loss
To love, is to risk not being loved in return
To live, is to risk dying; to hope is to risk despair
To try, is to risk failure
*Yet risks **must** be taken, for the greatest hazard in all of life, is to risk nothing*
*The person who risks nothing, **does** nothing, **has** nothing, and **is***

nothing;
They may avoid suffering and sorrow
*But they cannot **learn, feel, change, grow, live**, nor **love***
Chained by their attitudes, they are but a slave
They have forfeited their freedom
For only a person who risks, will ever truly be free

Author unknown

You will never learn to love (or even like) your mistakes until you change your information with regard to how you view them.

In your **Draft Action Plan:** write your answer to the following question... If you can't bring yourself to "love" your mistakes, what will you do to at least see them as **positive, important** aspects of your life from now on?

When I was doing my martial art training in Kowloon, my Grand Master told us that we had to spend a minimum of 3 hours a week – learning from nature. Being rather immature at the time I thought this was pretty stupid, and asked what that actually meant.

He said to "Become that which you are studying – for example – go and hug a tree and 'become' the tree. Feel what **it** is feeling, try to understand what is going on in its world until some day, you will feel something brush your arm and when you look up, you will find that a bird has landed in the tree." I turned to my friend Leo and said, "Sure – knowing my luck it just pooped on my arm."

So I went out and instead of hugging trees, I used them as imaginary opponents - kicking and punching them, and I "made up" lessons to bring back to the class.

Then one day I spotted an ant (they are quite large over there), with an insect about the size of a bumblebee that it was towing back to the nest. I have always been interested in insects and spiders and such, so I decided to try what my Master had said. I squatted down and tried to project myself into the ant, and to my surprise – I actually started to feel really good about myself as I thought about how happy the rest of the ants would be, at this big amount of food that I was bringing home.

Then the ant came up against a dirt mound (loose soil) - got part way up, and then slid back down. This went on for several minutes until I got **really** frustrated and jumped up and stormed off to go back and kick some more trees. I had only gone about ten paces when something happened. It was like something hit me in the back of the head and I just spun around and went right back there, before I really knew what was happening.

Over the next half hour or so, I went through every human emotion – the **hope** as he came back to try again, the **excitement** and **fear** (excitement as he got a little further up and the fear that he wouldn't make it), the **frustration**, the sense of **failure** as he appeared to give up and go to look for something else.

But he kept coming back, and finally – he got it over the top. I was so excited as I went back to share my "lesson" that my feet hardly seemed to touch the ground, but I wasn't really that sure of what the lesson actually was.

Finally – just as I was going through the door, the lesson came to me. It was, "There is no such thing as failure – only that you haven't found the way, and if you hang in there long enough and try hard enough – you **will** find a way.

When I left the navy with a trade but no formal educational qualifications, there were **so** many times when I sat back and thought "I just can't **do** this!" And every time that thought came – I saw my ant in my mind again and went back to work. As a result of what that ant taught me, I have achieved every business and personal goal that I have ever set for myself.

If I can learn something so important from an ant – what can I learn from **you**? What can **you** learn?

Exercise:

Take some time to enter into your **Personal Discoveries page**, "mistakes" that you have made in the past, and with this **new information** ask yourself if they really **were** mistakes, or opportunities that you overlooked.

In your **Draft Action Plan** note what you are going to do with future "mistakes" that you hope to make.

Chapter 6

NO SMALL THINGS

By "small," I mean all of those things that we see as too "small / little / inconsequential..." to be of any significance. One of the biggest "mistakes" we make in this life (remembering that the only true mistake is the one we haven't learned from) is seeing things as "small" or "insignificant," and it is the cause of many an argument between couples in particular. The female wants to be told regularly by her partner that she is loved, and the male doesn't get it – "What's the big deal? I told you when we got engaged and I'm still here aren't I? Go figure!"

By the end of this chapter you will be able to:

~ More readily identify those (previously) "small" things that are so very important in reality

~ List the "small" things in your life that you may have been inappropriately treating as insignificant, and

~ Measurably improve your relationships by paying more **attention** to those "small" things"

It is critical that we appreciate that there are **no** small or insignificant things really - **every one** of the biggest things in this world, is made up of "small" things. Think of the size of the seed that produces the mighty redwood tree. Too many "small" things pack an unbelievable punch - look at the size of the atom and the power of the explosion that it produces. And what about some of the viruses going round today?

Do you have any idea of what (indirectly) kills more people in the world each year than any other thing? Actually **cars** (and doctors) do pretty well but no, the answer I'm looking for is the **mosquito.** Small? Sure is. Insignificant? **No way!**

So what I'm **really** saying is there are **heaps** of "small things" in reality - they surround us. But if you want to start living the life you **really** want, then **never ever**, pass a "small" thing off as **insignificant,** until you've checked it out **thoroughly**! Men make that mistake **all** the time don't they ladies?

The number of people I have seen at their partner's funeral or hospital bed sobbing and saying "I didn't even tell him/her I loved him/her this morning;" would just rip your heart out.

Going back to the car - what would you say is the most important "thing" or part (as a generalization) - the engine, the wheels, the lights, the door handles, or the key?

The same is true of this manual - no **one** thing is more or less important than any other so please - take it **all**. You've paid for it, and **anything** you discard, leaves you with less of a "vehicle."

> The thing that scares me most about being human is the speed with which we move to complacency.
>
> *Tom Grbich*

The thing that scares me most about being human is the speed with which we move to complacency – a state that is especially well addressed by the "No Small Things" concept. I was raised close enough to the beach that I could have gone there every day by two-wheeler if I had wanted to.

Then my niece (7 years old) visited from the Philippines with her Mum, and we took them to Ninety Mile Beach in the far North of New Zealand.

In bare feet we walked down onto the sand and as my wife and her sister walked towards the water, I got the feeling that something was "happening" behind me. When I turned around – there was my little niece - absolutely rigid, and shaking all over with the excitement of standing ankle deep in the sand, for the first time in her life. It brought tears to my eyes and I made the determination right then, to never be complacent about anything again.

When we moved to Canada as a family, I made sure my wife couldn't work for the first six months (by not applying for residence until she arrived) because she desperately needed a rest, and I knew she wouldn't take one unless she had no choice.

In the free time available, she started spending time with the children at school, and on one occasion went on her first field trip with our daughter (9). At some point during the day, Lahia came back to give her Mum a huge hug and tell her it was "the happiest day of her life." My wife asked "Why?" and was told, "Because you're here."

9/11 – If you still haven't "got it" – consider this...

~ As you might know, the head of a company survived 9/11 because his son started kindergarten that day.

~ Another fellow survived because it was his turn to bring donuts.

~ One woman was late because her alarm clock didn't go off in time.

~ One was late because of being stuck on the NJ Turnpike because of an auto accident.

~ One person missed his bus.

~ One spilled food on her clothes and had to take time to change.

~ One's car wouldn't start.

~ One went back to answer the telephone.

~ One had a child that dawdled and didn't get ready as soon as he should have.

~ One couldn't get a taxi.

~ But the one that struck me most, was the man who put on a new pair of shoes that morning. He took the usual means to get to work but before he got there, he developed a blister on his foot.

He stopped at a drugstore to buy a Band-Aid, and that's why he's alive today.

"Small" things? Just consider the consequences.

So when you find yourself stuck in traffic, you miss an elevator, turn back to answer a ringing telephone - all the "little" things that may have frustrated the wrinkles out of you in the past - think to yourself, "this is exactly where I am meant to be at this moment."

Next time your morning seems to be going wrong, the children are slow getting dressed, you can't seem to find the car keys, you hit every traffic light... don't get mad or frustrated – think of it as a "little thing" that may be keeping you from a "bigger thing," that might have been something that you **really** would rather not have experienced.

Print out and read **"No Small Things** and **The Most Beautiful Flower"**

Action Plan: See if you can find at least **one** thing in **your** life, that you've been treating as "small" *(saying thank you / I love you / I'm sorry / kissing the kids goodnight when you tuck them in bed, kissing your partner goodbye when you leave for work, e.g.)* - write it down, and make a note of what you're going to do to change that.

Having done that – why stop there? Write down **all** the things that you've been treating as insignificant and change the whole lot of them!

Chapter 7

UNDERSTANDING NEEDS

Almost everything in this world starts with, or because of, a need.

An understanding of what needs are all about is an absolute must, if you hope to get the best out of your dealings with other people, and life. It is a critical part of understanding yourself, and why some things that seem to have no effect on others whatsoever, cause you to stress out.

In fact, perhaps the only categorical statement anyone will ever hear me make; is that virtually **every,** response or reaction you will **ever** get, from **any** person that you deal with, at **whatsoever** level in your life, will relate **directly** to what you have just done **with** or **to,** that person's **needs!!** (Or perhaps what someone else just did).

> Almost everything in this world starts with, or because of – a need.
>
> *Tom Grbich*

By the end of this chapter you will be able to:

~ Identify the difference between needs and wants

~ Describe what activities are most likely to result in reactions as opposed to responses

~ Relate the things that cause you to react rather than to respond in your day to day life and relationships, and

~ Describe the changes **you** will make to ensure that more people respond, rather than react to you

True 'needs' are those things that **sustain life** - coming in two forms - physical & emotional.

Physical needs are those that most notably sustain life (including clean air, warmth, clean water, movement, rest, and nutrition).

Wants are usually derived **from** needs, but they are **very** different animals.

I mentioned earlier that **all** responses/reactions come from what **you** do (or someone **else** has done), to the other person's needs at that time. If you look at the graphical representation of physical needs (below), the centre line represents needs being sufficient, but there's **no resilience.** (The needs could be moved up **or** down with minimal external change.)

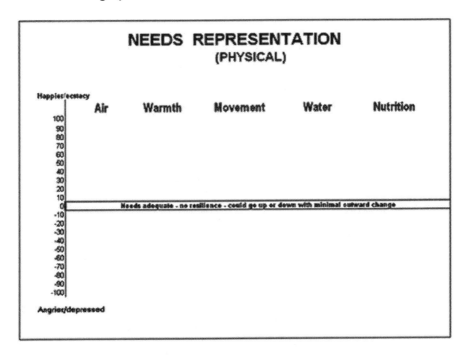

Now I know you wouldn't really **do** this but... jump into bed with your partner on a freezing winter's night and clamp your cold feet to the centre of their back. What do you think - bit of a reaction there?

Wrap someone in warm towels when they come in soaked to the bone from an unexpected winter's downpour, and the opposite is true.

I've arranged the physical needs in order of life threat. Cut off the oxygen supply to the brain and you've got about 60 seconds to live. Toss someone in the Arctic waters and I believe they have about 90 seconds. Tie a person in such a way that they can't move, and I've been told that survival is likely to be about two days (apparently the heart pumps the blood out but it's the squeezing action of muscles in movement that brings it back).

70

Deprive a person of water, and (depending on environmental conditions) they might last three to five days. Deprive them of nutrition, and I think the longest on record is ninety days, where all the other physical needs were catered for.

Emotional needs are more subtle (including respect/dignity, security, recognition, self-esteem, opportunity/achievement, direction, hope, freedom / independence, belonging / acceptance, love, and so on). Depriving or neglecting emotional needs **will kill you** just as surely - they just take a little longer.

Going back to our earlier question of "What does long term stress do to you" you will remember that the reptilian aspect of our brain (the part of the brain from which our instincts come), only understands **two conditions** - peace tranquility, joy, happiness (things are **ok**), and all the negative things; hatred, fear, guilt, insecurity, etc (things are **NOT** ok).

When we are "**not** ok" the brain prepares us for the "fight or flight" syndrome. Muscles tense to run or fight, nutrients are pulled back from the outer extremities of the body, the eyes dilate, pulse rate increases, adrenalin floods into the system and so on. Now those tensing muscles put pressure on the same nerves that I would use to treat illness in acupressure, or disable and perhaps even kill you, if I were fighting you. And adrenalin is toxic if not used.

The brain is therefore getting a **host** of erroneous messages, and will be activating glands whose services are not actually required. So in effect you're **poisoning** yourself.

One of the more immediate effects of the "not ok" situation is a measurable change in bowel movements (some people get diarrhoea – others become constipated), but I can assure you that there is a lot more untoward stuff going on in the background, that is potentially **much** more damaging.

Your whole immune system will ultimately suffer. You'll find yourself catching more colds and the dreaded flu, and ultimately **cancer** will begin to raise its ugly head. Have you ever noticed how sick days at work increase with the stress of what's going on at the time?

Quite apart from all of this, you won't be feeling that great mentally either, and thoughts can eventually turn suicidal. So if the **internal** damage doesn't kill you, what **you** do, might.

Material **wants** are very closely tied to our emotional needs - They're the desire for those material items that will compliment, bolster, or support our **emotional needs**, the more obvious of which include:

- **Respect/dignity** - what is **anyone** without respect? You can work, and even **live** with someone you don't love - but try living or working with someone you don't **respect.**

- **Recognition** - possibly one of the strongest needs - just watch children and how they clamour for attention with "Look Mum, watch me do this" (as they jump off a ledge that is one and half inches [3cm] high). Maturity tends to make us a **little** subtler about it, but the need is still there.

  In fact for those of you who are business people, an international survey many years ago indicated that the three most important things to people in the workplace were (in order)...

  1. Recognition
  2. A say (or shares) in the business, and
  3. Money

  Interestingly, where numbers one and two were not being satisfied, number three moved immediately to first place.

  Statistics tell us that something like **75%** of the world's population goes to bed hungry for **food** each night... but perhaps as many as **99%** of the world's population goes to bed each night, hungry for **recognition.** How sad is that?

- **Caring** - a world where no one cares is the loneliest of all places. I speak from experience here.

- **Importance** - who likes feeling that they don't count - that they have no value to the people or world around them?

- **Security** - how do you arrive at an "ok" situation when your life or belongings are insecure?

- **Self-acceptance/self esteem** - this need is not so obvious but it's also very powerful. Suicides and breakdowns come more from the inability to accept ourselves for what we are, than from any other reason. This is the playground of the ego and I'd like you to think about the insanity of it all. Who do you know that you would trust more (than you), who do you know that you would rather have as a friend than you? It just doesn't make sense!

~ **Direction** - more than half the problems of the business and natural worlds come from the lack of direction in people's lives. It contributes **tremendously** to insecurity and generally; a direction-less world is just a 'yucky' place to be.

~ **Opportunity** - life would be pretty depressing and hopeless if we did not have opportunities, to make the changes that we feel need to be made. Have you ever seen the effect on a friend when they saw themselves in a "hole" with no opportunity (in their mind) to get out? Not a pretty sight.

~ **Achievement** - in order to feel good within ourselves, we need to feel that we're achieving something.

~ **Belonging** - I speak from experience again when I say that if a world where no one cares is the loneliest **place** in the world, then feeling you don't **belong,** would have to be the loneliest **feeling** in the world.

~ **Freedom/independence** - freedom is perhaps the need that people are most willing to die for. To feel free to do and be what you want to do or be, is critical to self-esteem

~ **Acceptance** – we are a herd animal and our need for acceptance by our peers is strong. Fashion plays this need to tremendous advantage. Look at the terrible things women especially, have done to their bodies in order to be in "fashion." Over the centuries you've **poisoned** yourselves with body colouring that used arsenic as a base, you've ruined your backs with the shoes that you've worn and in China, women have been crippled, by the "need" to have small feet.

Men on the other hand, have died or been crippled carrying out acts of "bravado" that were nothing less than total idiocy - all in order to be accepted (and it still happens today)

~ **Equality** - no one enjoys being made to feel that they're inferior.

~ **Hope** - hope comes from the belief that one-day **some**how; things will change for the better. When you take away love - you trample a person's heart, when you take away hope - you trample their soul. Seeing opportunities with no hope of doing anything about them, is perhaps the most soul-destroying thing of all.

I want you to understand right now that there is no more important goal of this book than to give **you** back hope that is **real**.

You **can**, and you **will**, live the life you want, if you'll only go out and **make it happen**, using the tools you are being given here.

~ **Love** - unfortunately, so many of us never get to know what **true** love actually is. An interesting (if sometimes sobering) question to ask is, "Do I feel that I am truly loved?" Ask it now.

My wife is from the Philippines and she had been writing to several other people before we met, so the first thing I did on bringing her to New Zealand was to take her to meet those people. If she settled with me, I wanted her to be sure that I was the right choice. I didn't ever want her wondering if she would have been "better off," with one of them.

When we married, my "rule" was that she should never be made to feel uncomfortable in her own home by another person. So, whether it was one of my friends or a family member - if she felt uncomfortable with them in the house, then they would be advised that they could not come back. It didn't mean that I wouldn't continue to see them; I just wouldn't bring them home. (And "yes" the rule **was** applied to at least one person.)

One of my most treasured compliments came one night as we were driving home from visiting friends (about two years after we married). She suddenly turned to me and said "You know, when I got married I thought I was going to have to make all kinds of changes and compromises – but I feel more free now than I have ever felt in my life."

She also commented on how her friends at work talked about the compromises, "deals," and sacrifices they had to make in order to have their "girl's nights out," and they could not believe that **her** husband actually encouraged her, to go and have fun.

74

So let me assure you "true love" **does** exist, and my absolute recommendation to each and every one of you is - don't accept anything less. Appreciate that there is a difference however, between "true" love and "perfect" love. "Perfect love" is where everything is the way **you** want it to be and that is neither natural, healthy, nor likely.

As an example of the power of needs, if you have someone that you could work with right now − I'd like you to advise them that as an experiment, you are going to say something **really** mean to them and then discuss how they felt about what you said, (of course they have to imagine it is real).

It is not possible to be mean, without impacting negatively on their needs - but which ones did you drag down in particular? Discuss it with them and... apart from what he/she felt - how did **you** feel about what you did?

It's important to reverse that effect by making another statement now − telling them this is what you **really** think, and saying the nicest (genuine) thing, you can think of to them.

This time you have lifted their needs up and it will be interesting to know how they feel about the **real** statement − and how **you** now feel having said it.

If you can affect someone as powerfully as you did when they **knew** you were acting - can you begin to understand the incredible power this understanding will give you, to affect all the other people in your life?

In catering to people's emotional needs you achieve several things:

~   You make them feel **good**

~   You automatically gain their **respect** - and if you have their respect, they'll **trust** you.

~   You make them want to do something for **you** − (**everyone** likes feeling good), and

~   If you make people feel good, then they're going to feel comfortable with you.

Companies in monopoly situations make the mistake time and time again. They rip people off and provide lousy customer service – and how does that affect your need for dignity, respect, acceptance, and positive recognition? All this achieves is to **GUARANTEE** that one day they **WILL** have competition, and they **WILL** lose, far more customers than they ever needed to. **Think about it!**

When New Zealand opened the doors to airline competition, Ansett (who came in as a competitor) would surely have done their homework. If as a **result** of that research they had found that New Zealanders just **loved** their national carrier, they would have realised that the cost of gaining a foothold just may not have been worth it.

Another thing that amazes me is how banks abuse their customers. It is quite astounding that they have been effectively borrowing **your** money for 10, 20, even 30 years; using that money to make **very** good money for themselves, and they **charge** you for the privilege of helping them to make money? And let's say you've had two mortgages with them in that time - but who gets the good deals? You? Not likely. People who have never dealt with that bank in their **life**, are offered the special mortgage rates etc.

The fact is, if you're treating your customers with respect and integrity, you have **no need to fear** the advent of competition because even if someone else **does** start up, your losses will be minimal (as long as you don't get complacent). Typically you will only lose the customers that you would be glad to lose anyway, and the same goes for relationships.

AT THE SAME TIME YOU MUST NEVER NEGLECT YOUR OWN NEEDS!

If, in the process of catering to the needs of others you're neglecting your own needs, the toll **will** soon tell. If you're constantly putting aside your own need for self-respect, equality, etc. in order to please others, then you will soon become demotivated, irritable, the joy will disappear from your life, and ultimately, your health will follow. Frankly, it's just not worth it, and you're better off staying away from people who cause you to feel that way.

How do you take advantage of the opportunities that can come from this powerful information?

The first thing to appreciate is that we are **NOT** as different as some would like us to believe. I don't care what your race, nationality, religion, or creed... there is no (normal) person on this earth who **likes** to be treated disrespectfully, to have their dignity trampled on, to be outcast etc. **The needs I'm talking about are universal.**
I have no doubt that my understanding of needs and my acceptance of the fact that we are basically the same where needs are concerned, saved my life on at least half a dozen occasions in Asia.

As I mentioned earlier, my wife is from the Philippines. Having gone there to meet her, I suggested it would be sensible for her to come to New Zealand for a visit, to see whether or not it was a country she'd like to live in, before we looked at developing our relationship any further. She wrote back and advised that her Mother was afraid. The Philippine government had been running a program on television warning of the dangers of Philippine ladies marrying other nationalities, and the things that had been done to some of these ladies, were tragic.

With what we've learned - what would her Mum's needs graph have looked like do you think? What would **you** *have done to assuage that?*

I wrote back and told Susan not to worry - that I'd write to her Mum. In my letter to Mrs. Basilio I asked her to put her religion and culture aside and answer some basic questions. I discussed the concerns and wishes that **my** Mum would have if my sister was going to the Philippines, and asked if there was any difference to the fears and hopes that she had for Susan. I told her that if my sister was considering marrying a person of **whatever** nationality she would hope to be treated with respect and dignity, she would hope that he would be loving and kind, and that he would help her on her journey through life. I asked if there was anything different that Susan might be wanting of a husband.
Susan's Mum wrote back agreeing that we're not that different, and giving her blessing to Susan coming to NZ. So Susan came, thankfully she stayed, and life has got better ever since.

How do you get to become good at this? When you've accepted the "needs concept" as fact, start by analysing situations. When you overhear a conversation and you feel that little unpleasantness in the pit of your stomach, ask yourself, "which of the needs of the person being spoken to, just got lowered somewhat." Equally, when you feel uplifted or see another person uplifted by something that someone else said or did, ask the question again about which of the needs got a boost and why.

Start looking at people and trying to pick which of their needs may need a boost, and then try it. In no time at all you'll find your accuracy improving out of sight and you'll find yourself getting more and more, out of life.

When people attack **your** needs; before reacting - ask what in **their** needs chart might be causing their behaviour, and with your new knowledge - what might **you** be able to do to change that?

This new insight will also give you far greater understanding of yourself and your moods, and you'll be on the road to learning how to "choose your day" by choosing what things are allowed to affect you, and how. You have begun "taking your power back."

To give you an indication as to how this works in a real situation, let's say I'm selling a unit costing tens of thousands of dollars to a small to medium sized company in hard times - something that could make or break the company. Can you imagine the power of my saying "Karen, I wonder what the impact would be, of your making a **wrong** decision on this system?" All of a sudden she's going to be grabbing for her oxygen mask and the escape handles isn't she? Why? What need/s have I just awakened? *(Security, value as an employee, the need for respect... and so on, come to mind)*

Now we're dealing with the **real** issue - her need for job security will potentially be the most powerful driver of all, so all I actually have to **sell** her on, is that the **only** possible impact of buying from me is to make her look good in the eyes of the company as a whole.
One of the most powerful advertisements I have ever seen, came out just after the share-market crash in the 80s. IBM presented a plain blue screen while making this simple statement in its ad. - "No one **ever** got fired, for buying IBM." Nothing else - that's all it said. But

can you imagine how that advertisement impacted on the need for security in some **incredibly** insecure times, of someone who'd just been tasked with sourcing and buying some computers?

If you have heard of the "Secret," you will be aware of perhaps **the** most powerful marketing campaign of all. Think of the word "secret" and all that it implies (from a "needs" perspective). If you are "in" on the secret then you are special. If you don't know the secret then you are not, so right away – people's attention has been engaged.

Then, the marketing goes on to suggest that this information has been buried, suppressed, hidden..." and it even shows the words coming up on a typewriter suggesting that this information will "never be made available to the public."

It's the biggest load of crocodile dung that I've heard in a long time – the information has **never** been a secret, it has **never** been buried, suppressed, hidden or **any** of that garbage - but by far the bigger part of the population won't even consider that. The desire to be one of the "special" people who know the "secret," and the fury over such important information having been kept from them overrides all logic, and they want it whether they need it or not.

Although I abhor the deliberate, untruthful manipulation – I can't help admire the impact that it has effected.

All you need to do now is practise practise practise, and you'll find interactions with others at all levels, becoming easier, with every day.

EXERCISE:
1. Print off the **EmotionalNeeds** chart and draw your own graph to find out where your personal "sensitive" spots are, then

2. Go back to Chapter 4 ("What It Is To Be Human") and see what impact unfulfilled needs might have been having there.

3. What will you do to ensure that you get more responses from the people in **your** life from now on?

Chapter 8

DEALING WITH STRESS/HOW TO RELAX

The purpose of this section is to draw your attention to the things in your life that stand in the way of relaxation, and to question whether stress is necessarily a "bad" thing.

Introduction

In view of the fact that "Needs" often feature so strongly where stress is involved, there will be some "crossover" between the last chapter and this one.

Interestingly, most people think they are stressed because they don't have enough "balance" in their lives. If you are one of these people, take a glass and lay it on its side, then balance a knife, a spoon, a pen or whatever, on the side of the glass. Now what do you see happening? Nothing? Yes that's about right – so, is that how you want to spend the rest of your life? With nothing happening?
I would hope not.

It is also fascinating to me that there must be a thousand or more courses or programs "out there" - aimed at teaching you how to "manage" stress. Now what sort of insanity is that? Manage it? If you don't **like** stress then why on earth would you want to "manage" it? Why not get **rid** of it entirely (**deal** with it)?

Am I saying that you can get rid of **all** of the stress in your life? **No**! Why would you want to **do** that? Not **all** stress is bad (is it?). The stress that gets you moving – to do something important that you have been putting off, is **good** stress, and why would you want to get rid of that?

By the end of this chapter you will:

~   List the main causes of stress for you Relate whether (or where) your stress is a good or bad thing for you

~   Relate what long term stress does to a person

~   Identify the primary contributors to your stress by revisiting your "needs graph", and

~   Draw the (needs) graphs of others who are important to you

So, what causes stress? There are lots of things that **appear** to be the "cause" of stress but the overriding element behind that apparent "cause," will almost always be **fear** (often based in doubt). Let's take a look at some of the more common "stressors:"

~   Low self esteem - fear

~   Security - fear

~   Kids - fear

~   Judgement - fear

~   Guilt – fear

~   Not enough time - fear

~   Money - fear

~   Not taking responsibility

~   Relationships – often made more difficult because of inherent fears

~   No power to change things - fear

~   Work - fear

~   Non-achievement - fear

~   Over achievement - fear

~   Lack of direction

~   Lack of education – fear

~   Confrontation - fear

~   Lack of sleep

~   Change - fear

~   No balance in your life, and

~   As you saw in the previous chapter – unfulfilled needs

The list goes on and on – if there is one thing that almost everyone on the **planet** is incredibly good at it – it's "finding something to stress about."

What **is** fear (somebody said "False-Evidence-Appearing-Real")?

Whatever you may call it, it is a **symptom** (just like stress) - of many things e.g. insecurity (lack of confidence in your ability to fulfill the more important of your needs perhaps?), failure, tense environments, confrontation etc. - all coming back to... how you **THINK**!

Quote: *"Fear is that little darkroom where negatives are developed."* *Originator unknown.*

Low self esteem – the fear here is that we are not worthy of other people's respect, friendship, caring etc, that we won't be able to do the job as well as someone else... blah, blah, blah.

> It **ALL** comes down to...
> "How you think."
>
> *Tom Grbich*

Security – we're afraid that someone will attack us, rob us, we'll lose our job, things aren't going well at work, maybe our partner doesn't **really** love us, we might get sick, have an accident... blah, blah, blah.

Kids – we're afraid that they won't do well at school, someone will introduce them to drugs, they'll get pregnant (or get someone **else** pregnant), they'll have an accident, get sick, there'll be a war and they'll have to go fight in some country we haven't even read about, they'll be kidnapped... blah, blah, blah.

Judgement – we're afraid that we won't measure up to someone else's standards, or **we** are judging others and knowing that's not a nice thing to do – we feel "bad about that"... blah, blah.

Guilt – we did something that we're not particularly proud of and we're afraid someone will find out, or that we will have to "pay" in some way.

Money – there'll **never** be enough! Fear that someone will sue us; we'll lose everything we have – won't be able to pay the bills, won't be able to put food on the table... blah, blah, blah.

And so it goes on – it's all "blah," and notice how often the **real** issue is fear? But I did ask the question – is all stress/fear bad? Once again it comes down to how you "see" it (how you think). If you see it as bad then bad it will be, but – it doesn't **have** to be that way.

Fear

Our deepest fear is not that we are inadequate
Our deepest fear is that we are powerful beyond measure
It is our light, not our darkness that most frightens us
We ask ourselves, who am I to be brilliant, gorgeous, talented,
fabulous?

Actually, who are you NOT to be? You are a child of the Universe.
Your playing "small" does not serve the world.
There is nothing enlightened about "shrinking" so that other people
won't feel insecure around you.

We were born to manifest the glory of the "God" that is within us. It is
not just in some of us... it is in EVERYONE and as we let our own light
shine, we unconsciously give other people permission to do the same.
As we are liberated from our own fear, our presence automatically
liberates others.
Nelson Mandela?

So, who is the all time promoter and supporter of fear – of course –
our 'friend' the ego.

What things cause the most stress to you personally? Think about it
and write everything that comes to mind, in your "**Things to Work
On**" page.

Revisit your own "needs graph" on the "**Emotional Needs**" chart to
better recognise and understand your most sensitive areas, and feel
free to make copies so you can draw the graphs of other people who
are important to you.

Looking at your graph, are you able to get an appreciation now, of
why certain things have been or continue to be, stressful for you?
Look for needs that are important to you and which are closer to (or
below) the median line.

What will you do (**Draft Action Plan**) to build some strength into
those areas and if you 'don't know' what to do – who will you ask?

Can you see areas where **you** may have been causing stress for
other people?

How are you going with your plan to get more responses and fewer reactions, from the people in your life?

Remember what long-term stress does to you? Not only is stress the **number one** cause of cancer in women around the world today, some believe it's the number one cause of **all** illness! I did my own little survey recently and **every single person that I know** who has **had** cancer, **has** cancer, or has **died** of cancer, was, or is, stressed (a worrier).

When counselors tell you that in order to get rid of the stress in your life you have to "let things go" or "forgive and forget," they are talking absolute nonsense. It is not **possible** to "let worries/stresses "go." Go where?

The next time a counselor tells you that – withhold payment for your next three visits and ask them to demonstrate, by letting **that** go.

It's like me saying a crazy word like "noffstruckle" and telling you to "forget you ever heard it." Ridiculous!

So if you have struggled with "letting things go" in the past – don't beat yourself up over it – **celebrate** – you're **normal** because it can't be done. Anything put into your mind is there forever (remember that), but it **can** be disempowered. You can't take it out, but you **can** take its power away.

There are only two ways in which to truly deal with the things that have stressed you out in the past (and perhaps currently).

1. Change the way you **deal** with them, and that will happen when you can **change your information** – i.e. the way you "see" them, or

2. Disempower them by getting them **out of your system**. While they are **inside** you – **you** are part of the problem. Write them down and then burn the paper after agreeing with yourself that once they're on that paper – **they are no longer part of you.** The **memory** of the problem will forever remain, but the power that the problem had **over** you, is gone.

After my family joined me in Canada, I experienced the toughest two years I have ever experienced in a relationship with my partner.

Usually I am very quick to take action in such situations, based on my formula...

~   If you don't like the environment that you are living/working in

~   You have done everything you can do to change it but you don't have the authority, power... whatever is needed to make the changes you desire, and

~   The person who **could** change it – won't, then

~   You have two choices

Those two choices are:

1.   Leave, or

2.   Stay, and forfeit whining rights

On this occasion I felt that leaving was not to be my path, (but neither was living in an unhappy environment). I really did **not** enjoy the constant barbs being fired at me and therein was my answer. I had to "change my information" – meaning that somehow, I had to change how I viewed the "barbs." If you really 'listen' to your own words – it is fascinating how often they will provide your solution.

After (**considerable**) contemplation I was drawn to one of my own strongest beliefs - that hardship and mistakes provide the two greatest learning opportunities in this lifetime, and I realised that I was being a total fraud – I wasn't practicing what I preached.

If I truly believed my own (often repeated) statement that "learning is the best reason for being here" then how could I feel resentful, bitter, frustrated, and angry towards the person who was giving me some of the best (albeit toughest) learning opportunities of my life? And the 'righteous logic' of the ego was right behind me here – I was a good husband in every way, I didn't deserve to be treated like this... blah blah blah – urging me to make a bad decision.

So I changed my perception (my information) – visualising the "barbs" coming from her mouth turning to "gifts" (of learning) before they struck, and my whole world changed in the process.
With every learning situation there is a "learning curve" however. As you reach the top of the curve you don't stop learning, but the amount of learning gained for the time spent diminishes, and you

have to consider whether or not you are still getting value. Ultimately therefore, I reached the peak of the learning curve (as we do), and on one occasion as my wife was slashing me with her tongue once again, I smiled at her and said, "You know, one day you will probably cause me to leave you, but the one thing I will **never** allow you to do – is to stop me loving you." That stopped her in her tracks and two days later she came to me and in her own words, she told me, "I've decided to stop being such a bitch."

Life has just got better and better ever since, and we are happier together than we have ever been.

Forgiving
Often we are told that the only way to truly set ourselves free is to learn to "forgive." **I disagree**. As I implied earlier – judging is "God's" job (however you see God) so (in my perception) that makes forgiving "wrong." Why do I say that? Well in order to forgive don't you first have to **judge** that the other person did something wrong?
Is it any wonder that people are stressed when psychiatrists and other "do-gooders" have told us that in order to be a "good person" we have to "forgive and forget, turn the other cheek" etc? And what happens when we just can't seem to bring ourselves to do that? Yup – stress comes racing in through that wide open door – we're "baaadddd" people.

When my Mum died, the remaining family came together in a way that it never had before, but it didn't take long at all for my father to split us up again, by challenging the will (even implying that they had not legally divorced). As we left the lawyer's office after coming to a final agreement, he asked "Where does this leave us then?" I told him he had made his choice with his final actions and there no longer **was** an "us." I did not want him in any part of my life ever again.

He responded with – "Well the least you could do is to forgive me" and my reply was – "There is nothing to forgive. In order to forgive you, I would have to judge you as having done something wrong, and that is not my place. Whether I agree with your behaviour or not, you (albeit unwittingly) played a big part in making me the person I am today, and how could I be angry with you for that? What I **am** prepared to judge though is the fact that (in my perception), you have never brought anything positive into my life, and I just choose not to have people like that, **in** my life any longer."

So he is now just another person that I once knew, who is no longer a part of my life, and I feel very, very good about that. The best part is that I have no stress, no self - judgment, no struggle to "let it go," no guilt, and no need to "forgive" anyone.

The one judgment that is our absolute right to make – is to judge that we do or do not like what a person or circumstance brings into our lives, and to act on that judgment. In fact we **must** make that judgment in order to get rid of the negatives. Be very clear however that it is the behavior, situation or circumstance that we judge – **not** the person.

Dealing with the symptoms

Because I've agreed that none of us has wings yet, I have to accept that it's unlikely that anyone is going to be able to make an instant change to a stress-free life. So let's talk about some methods for relieving stress **symptoms** in the meantime (and I'm sorry but alcohol and drugs won't be on the list!)

~ Breathing – by far the most powerful stress reliever ever - is (proper) breathing. Close your eyes (if possible – you don't **have** to) and focus at the bottom of your belly. Breathe in through the nose and fill your lungs from the bottom to the top, then slowly release the air. As the air enters your body, imagine that it is mixing with all the toxicity inside (body and mind) and taking that toxicity out as it leaves. Each new breath has less toxicity to mix with, so in no time at all you will feel fresh, stress-less, and back in control. It is free, and the only side effects are relaxation, refreshment, and release from whatever was bugging you. A bargain in anyone's language!

~ Exercise, meditation, yoga, Tai Chi, pressure points, hypnosis, walks in nature, the beach, music etc. are all excellent stress relievers - choose the one that fits best with "you."

Dealing with the cause/s

It's important that you are comfortable with the concept of fear being the main cause of stress. If not – find someone to discuss it with until you can at least accept it as a very good place to start.

How do we deal with **fear** then? Most often, fear comes from a lack of information, misunderstanding, and/or (**especially**) - **imagination**. Ignorance is an **incredible** fear driver, it's the basis of all superstition, and the imagination can make the least scary thing in the world, seem like the worst.

Public speaking is a perfect example. As far as can be told, only one person in the history of public speaking has ever died while doing it (had a heart attack apparently), and absolutely **no one** has ever been injured by it (although in the past some may have been injured by the **audience,** disagreeing with what they said). And yet it is scary enough for many, to induce loss of voice, the need for an **immediate** washroom break, and almost instant nausea – even vomiting.

It is insane, most people would rather jump in a car and drive a thousand miles in the worst traffic than give a fifteen minute speech, yet the likelihood of horrific injury and even death while on the road is **so** much greater, there is no comparison. This is the work of the ego again.

Years ago, I realised that fear of the unknown was preventing me from becoming a sales person so I undertook to learn all I could about what the sales role entailed.

I would accost people wearing suits and carrying briefcases in the street, to ask if they were in sales and what that entailed if they were. I read books, and considered what skills and qualities might be most important. The knowledge gained reduced my fears and then I applied for a job, having realised that there was nothing about the role that I could not do (however ineptly). I subsequently went on to make the top 1% in the world with a 91% closing rate, in one twelve month period – imagine the waste if I had allowed fear to keep me down.

The best way to deal with fear is to gather all the information possible about that thing that you fear, talk to others about it, and then just **do** it.

In summary:

~   When the oxygen masks fall in an aeroplane – remember whose mask you put on first. You are of no use to anyone if you are not breathing, so – consider other people's needs in everything you do, but **never** lose sight of your own.

~ The closer your need satisfaction level sits to the median line, the less it takes to pull it down to where the problems start. Think of those people who burst into tears at the tiniest little thing and appreciate, that there is virtually no tolerance left in their need satisfaction levels, and

~ Appreciate that **needs change** – with life, age and circumstances. Re-draw your needs graph as often as appropriate, so that you don't get hit from behind.

Exercise:
Having drawn your own needs graph, write those needs that are most important to you in your **Personal Discoveries Page**, and do whatever you can to provide more fulfillment, or to gain strength in those areas.

Not only will it help you, but it will help others too, because they won't have to be so sensitive around you.

Chapter 9

EFT

Sometimes, knowing "what" we need to do, "why" we need to do it, and even "how" to do it – is still not enough. If you know what, why and how but you're still having trouble with "do," there may be a deep underlying cause that needs to be ferreted out (something is standing in the way), and EFT (is often a great tool for doing that.

EFT is a "Whole Person" treatment system that is providing astounding results all over the world in dealing with pain, trauma, addiction, phobias and so on. The acronym stands for Emotional Freedom Technique although I believe "Energy Clearing Technique" better describes what it actually does.

The technique works on the principle that we are multi faceted beings - physical, mental, emotional, and spiritual but most importantly - the concept that we are a spirit with a body - not the other way around. The spiritual part of course is the "energy" side of us. EFT is intended to cover the "whole" being.

By the end of this chapter you will be able to:

~ Explain in your own words, what EFT is all about

~ Describe why it works where so often, everything else has failed

~ Describe the physical treatment technique, and

~ Begin using it safely, on yourself and others

Introduction

When we sustain an "injury," one or more aspects of our "self" is affected but in **all** cases, the impact will be felt in our "energy." Particularly traumatic experiences can trigger **major** disruptions in our "energy," which often don't go away by themselves. The crux of this is that you may attempt to heal the other elements but if you don't treat the energy disruption, the best that you can hope for from any other treatment, is temporary relief.

To explain this further – when something important or serious happens, we are impacted on many dimensions. If you seriously cut your leg for example – the physical energy has obviously been impacted. The cut will have affected at least one of the energy meridians of the body, and if the cut is serious then you will have been impacted mentally as you thought "Oh my God – what have I done?" Equally, you will almost certainly have been affected emotionally too, as you 'fear' what the end consequences of the wound might be.

Typically though – the only thing we treat is the actual physical wound, and we hope the rest will look after itself. This rarely happens in reality however, and amputation is a great example of that. Many if not all people who have a limb amputated, will feel pain in the limb that no longer exists. This pain is very real and can even require medication to cope with. The reason 'phantom limb pain' exists is because we have only dealt with the physical aspect of the injury. EFT has proven to be extremely effective in removing phantom limb pain (as has acupuncture)

So this technique literally relates the complaint whatever it may be, back to the energy level and when the energy disruption is removed, (often) so is the symptom.

It's not a case of "healing your energy" (my belief) - energy as we know, is indestructible, so why would it need healing? I see this more as a case of "restoring" the energy to its natural flow, or removing the aberrations.

It may be the only truly holistic treatment used today...

~ The physical element of the treatment comes from the physical contact of the "tapping."

~ The mental aspect of the problem is addressed by a statement that accurately describes the problem (or its symptoms).

~ The emotional aspect is addressed by visualising the experience or another experience like it (engaging with it), or by strongly emoting with your statement and giving it real power, and

~ The "energy" element is dealt with by the fact that the physical tapping is carried out on specific "meridian" points.

In many instances the cure is immediate, lasting, and complete. It is often truly mind boggling - seeming to work equally well on physical, mental, **and** emotional issues.

Note that all of the following must be carried out with a specific issue needing to be resolved, in mind.

The Basic Recipe
1. Repeat an affirmation 3 times while you...

2. Rub the sore spot (Yingchang [ST16 on an acupuncture chart] half way between the centre of the collar bones and the nipple [of a firm breast]) or alternatively tap the "Karate chop" point (the centre of the part of the hand that would strike in a Karate chop). Note that either one of the ST16 points can be used – you don't need both.
    As with acupressure, the amount of pressure applied should create discomfort rather than pain and after one or two sessions typically, the "sore spot" will not be uncomfortable any longer.

If using the Karate chop point, tap vigorously with the index and middle fingers of the dominant hand. Either side works but if applying the method to yourself, you will usually find that the dominant hand is easier to control in the tapping. Once again, the level of tapping should not cause pain and considering that the cause of psychological issues often involves negative thinking, it should be no surprise that the correction for it includes a neutralizing affirmation as follows:

Even though I have this _____, I deeply and completely accept myself.

The blank is filled in with a brief description of the problem that you want to address. Here are some examples...

Even though I have this fear of public speaking, I deeply and completely accept myself.

Even though I have this headache, I deeply and completely accept myself.

Even though I have this anger towards my father, I am a good and worthy person.

Even though I have this war memory, I deeply and completely accept myself.

Even though I have this stiffness in my neck, I deeply and completely accept myself.

Even though I have these nightmares, I deeply and completely accept myself.

Even though I have this craving for alcohol, I deeply and completely accept myself.

Even though I have this fear of snakes, I know they don't really want to hurt me.

Even though I have this depression, I deeply and completely accept myself.

This is only a partial list, of course, because the possible issues that are able to be addressed by EFT are endless.

The *"deeply and completely accept myself"* part can be changed too although it works well in almost every instance. For example, you could say... *"Even though I have this fear of public speaking, I know I am going to ace it."*

I realised that something was bothering my (13 year old) daughter one day and with questioning, it came out that other kids were calling her "fat." She was about 5 or ten pounds (2-5Kg) overweight at the time so I suggested we use EFT to deal with it.

Using the statement "Even though kids are calling me fat, I deeply and completely accept myself" brought the impact down only about 3 points – it wasn't really working and I felt she wasn't really engaging) emoting with the statement.

So I suggested "Let's try a different statement – let's go with Even though kids are calling me fat, they're just jealous cos I'm such a hot chick!" She wrapped herself around that one immediately and her distress was gone in one session.

See if you can come up with some statements that you would like to try later.

Sequence

Having completed this part you are now ready to move to the second part of the treatment, which Involves tapping typically 5 to 9 times on each of the following points in sequence...

EB - Eyebrow – tap at the start of the eyebrow - nearest the nose. (Bladder 2)

SE - Side of the eye – tap on the bone at the side of the eye. (Gall bladder 1) **UE** - Under the eye – tap about one inch down from the pupil (when looking straight ahead). (Stomach 2)

UN - Under the nose (Nasion) – tap in the centre of the upper lip, between the lip and the nose. (Governing vessel 26)

Chin - Midway between the bottom of the chin and the top of the bottom lip.

Collarbone - Tap between the collarbone and the first rib where they meet at the breastbone. (Kidney 27)

UA - Under the arm at the side/s of the body, about four inches (10Cm) below the armpit (in line with the nipple on a man's breast). (Spleen 18)

BN - Approx one inch below the nipple on men – base of the breast for women. (Stomach 18)

TH - On the thumb at the outside of the thumbnail

IF - On the thumb side of the index finger – level with the base of the nail.

MF - On the thumb side of the middle finger – level with the base of the nail.

LF - On the thumb side of the little finger – level with the base of the nail.

KC - On the "Karate chop" point of the hand.

To summarise the points in sequence, they are...

-	EB	Eyebrow
-	SE	Side of the eye
-	UE	Under the eye
-	UN	Under the nose (nasion)
-	Chin	Chin
-	Collarbone	Under the collarbone, against the sternum
-	UA	Under the arm
-	BN	Below the nipple

- ST	Side of the thumb
- SI	Side of the index finger
- SM	Side of the middle finger
- SL	Side of the little finger
- KC	Karate chop point

Brain alignment point

To enhance the overall effectiveness of the treatment (this is not necessary but is helpful), it is sometimes worth doing the set-up (1 & 2 under "The Basic Recipe), completing the sequence, going through the process below, and doing the sequence once again.

The Gamut point is the point at the back of the hand between the little finger and the next finger (TH 3).

The purpose of using this point is to fine-tune the mind to the procedures being used. While tapping the gamut point continuously, the following actions should be carried out...

1. Close eyes
2. Open eyes
3. Look hard down and to the right without moving the head.
4. Look hard down and to the Left without moving the head.
5. Roll the eyes in a circle like the "second" hand of a clock.
6. Repeat number five in the opposite direction.
7. Hum any song for 2 seconds (e.g. The first line of "Happy Birthday").
8. Count rapidly from one to five.
9. Hum 2 seconds of a song again
10. Repeat the tapping sequence.

Reminder phrase

Often the success of the system is enhanced considerably by reminding yourself of the problem being dealt with at each tapping point. The whole affirmation does not need to be repeated – egg. If the affirmation were "Even though I have this stiffness in my neck, I deeply and completely accept myself," as you tapped on each sequential point, you would only need to repeat, "Stiff neck."

This is most times not necessary, but when it **is** necessary, it is **really** necessary so until you are really skilled at determining which is which, it is just as easy to include it.

Repeat sessions

Where repeat sessions are necessary (for the same complaint), it is critical that you adjust the affirmations to suit. For example, using the statement... *"Even though I have this stiffness in my neck, I deeply and completely accept myself"* - in repeat sessions (where the problem hasn't entirely gone) you would change the statement to... *"Even though I have some remaining stiffness in my neck, I deeply and completely accept myself."*

The reminder phrases should also change to "remaining stiffness" e.g.

Testing

It is very helpful to evaluate the extent of a problem on a scale of 0 to 10 (where 10 represents maximum intensity and 0 represents no intensity whatsoever). This provides a benchmark against which to measure progress. You might start at a 6, for instance, and then go to a 3... and then a 1... and finally to 0... as various rounds of The Basic Recipe are applied.

You should always measure the intensity, as it exists NOW... as you think about it... and not as you think it would be in the actual situation. Remember, The Basic Recipe balances the disruptions in your energy system, as they exist NOW while you are tuned in to the thought or circumstance. Here's an example of how it works.

Let's say you have a fear of spiders that you would like to put behind you. If there is no spider present to cause you any emotional intensity then close your eyes and imagine seeing a spider or imagine a past time when a spider scared you. Assess your intensity on a scale of 0 to 10, as it exists NOW while you think about it. If you estimate it at a 7 for example, then you have a benchmark against which to measure your progress.

Now do one round of The Basic Recipe and imagine the spider again. If you can get no trace whatsoever of your previous emotional intensity then you are done. If, on the other hand, you go to, let's say, a 4 then you need to perform subsequent rounds until 0 is reached.

Parameters

It is important to note that different presentations of the same thing may change the parameters. For example, if the thought of the spider was of a stationery spider and you are then presented with a moving spider, the original fear may surface at full strength. These parameters must be considered in any treatment.

Specificity
It is equally important to be extremely specific in dealing with a problem where possible. "I want to improve my self image" is non-specific and cannot be treated in its generalized form. In order to improve self-image, you must break down the elements that contribute to your low self-image and as you deal with each of these elements, so can you expect a result.

Interestingly the technique will sometimes still work even in the event that you can't be as specific as we would like. For example... *"Even though I don't know what is wrong with me, I ..."*

General note:
In by far the majority of cases, measurable (lasting) success will be gained with just one treatment. In the few instances where it isn't, it is well worthwhile going back to your questions to see if there may be other underlying causes... some things can run very deep.

For more information, check out the EFT website...
http://www.emofree.com/default.htm and don't hesitate to contact a registered practitioner for more serious issues.

Example:
As an example of the amazing power of EFT, I had a young lady come to me with severe panic attacks. She had been on medication for two years and disillusioned with the side effects, she had come off the drugs. That (naturally) swung the pendulum hard over, and she was having difficulty in dealing with life.

I asked her what would typically trigger a panic attack, and she advised that flying was a guarantee – and she already had her tickets to begin her overseas adventure in ten days time.

Measure
As a measure, I asked her to imagine that she was boarding a plane right then, hearing the whining of the engines, surrounded by other

passengers etc. To my horror, her pulse rate went from 72 to 180 and climbing, in less than a minute. That was **dangerous** so I shut that experience down **real** quick and we began the process... "Even though I have this crippling fear of flying – I deeply and completely accept myself" while massaging the "sore point."

Then we moved on to the tapping with her repeating "Fear of flying" with each point.

At the end of the sequence we did do the brain alignment process, and then repeated the tapping sequence.

With considerable trepidation at the end of the second sequence, I tried the experiment again and after some moments she looked strangely at me and said "This is spooky – I can't make myself scared." We were able to alter her heart rate by only about three beats per minute.

In view of the severity of the problem I suggested that we do another session before she boarded her plane, and that session turned out to be little more than a joke. She laughed most of the way through, and the last I heard from her was via an email from Thailand, where she said she had had the best plane trip of her life.

Chapter 10

LOVE & RELATIONSHIPS

Perhaps the least understood of the "most important things" in our world, is love. It just doesn't make sense that something so beautiful is so often the cause of more pain, sadness, and low self-esteem, than anything else I can think of. "True" love seems surrounded by almost endless confusion – much of which is created by the thousands of fairytale romance novels around the world.

In fact – even the words "true love" are confusing – if it's love - it **is** true – there **is** no "false love" because if it's false, then it's not love – is it?

Objective

By the end of this chapter you will be able to:

~ Identify what love is, as opposed to what love is not

~ Separate the confusion between "sex" and "love"

~ Define what love "looks like" to you

~ More accurately evaluate your own feelings

~ Describe the "symptoms" of real love (know when love is beginning in you), and

~ List questions that you will ask before entering into your next long-term relationship

Sometimes it's easier to look at what something is **not,** and that's where I am going to start with this one.

Love is **not:**

~ "One off" (or "one chance" only)

~ Sex

~ Romance

~ Desire

~ A need

~ Conditional, or

~ "Ownership"

Love is not "one off" – what I mean by this is that you don't just get "one shot" at love in your lifetime. It is **entirely** possible (and normal) to love more than one person, and lots of "things" – all at the same time even!

Love comes in many forms – there is the love for a pet, for a "thing" (a car, a motorbike, a home or a place e.g.), there is the love for your child, your parents (sometimes), a brother or sister (sometimes), a friend, food (oh yeah!!) and of course - your life partner if you're lucky enough to find such a person.

> It is **entirely** possible to love more than one person, and lots of "things" – all at the same time.
>
> *Tom Grbich*

Love has no limitations – when you think there's just no "room" to love anyone else, or to love someone even more – you'll be constantly amazed to find that the "room" actually, has no walls.

It is important to appreciate that you can experience the same **amount** of love for each **of** your "loves" individually – but how that love **affects** you, will be different for each one. You can love two or more children, friends, pets etc. every bit as much as the other – and there is nothing "wrong" with that.

The concept that there is only one ideal partner in this world of X billion people, is insane. Friends of my parents had the nearest thing to "perfect love" that I have ever seen and when the husband died at quite a young age, the wife deteriorated rapidly. It was only her teenage son and daughter that kept her alive and I remember my Mum saying many times over – "She'll never find another one like Baden."

Mum was right – she didn't find one like Baden – she found someone entirely different, but she told my Mum that to her amazement, she loves him just as much. He will never **replace** Baden in her heart and no "new" partner should be expected to do that. This is an entirely new and **different** love, and life.

The great thing about love is that there is absolutely no limit to its capacity.

Sex - one of the most seriously misleading and damaging elements of the romance novels worldwide, is their seeming inability to separate love from sex, and unfortunately, young girls are the ones most likely to **read** these stupid novels - at a time when they're most vulnerable (and impressionable).

They even call the sexual act "making love," yet that act very often has no recognisable elements of love in it. In the extreme circumstance - think about rape for example. Sex in **any** form where one party feels that they really didn't want it (even if they didn't fight it), is a control or self gratification issue, and there can be no "love" for the other person in that! And where do love and sex go together in the act of masturbation, or sex with blow up dolls, sex toys, and/or animals?

They **can** go together, and when they do it's a truly wonderful experience but if you expect them to automatically **fit** together, you are setting yourself up for a lot of confusion, disappointment, and potential pain.

> The "best sex" you will ever have, may very likely be with someone you do not "love."
>
> *Tom Grbich*

The best sex you will ever have, may very likely be with someone you don't love. Equally, if sex comes to an end through injury, age or whatever – does that mean the "love" is gone? Not if it is real, I can assure you.

Boys use the confusion to put unbelievable pressure on girls – "If you **really** loved me you'd go to bed with me..." The girl's heart tells her she really **does** love him – so why is there this reluctance to "**make** love?" The reality is – if the boy really loved **her** – he wouldn't push for something that she is not ready to do yet. Girls also become trapped in the concept that if she allows a guy to have sex with her, **then** he will love her.

Not a chance! Most times by far, once the guy has got what he wants – he's off to the next encounter! Unfortunately for the female, the act of sex often **confirms** her **love** for him, while for the guy, it confirms that it was just **lust**.

Romance – romance is another thing that goes beautifully **with** love but is **not** "love" per se. Romance is the act, art, or process of **convincing** a person that you love them, and it can be incredibly deceitful - often being applied only to "get what you want" from the other person. This fascinating art is a perfect complement to love, but it has been used to lure many a person to their death over the centuries

Desire – desire often comes **from** love but it is **not** love in itself. Desire is just an intensely strong wish to fulfill a momentary need, or an immensely strong attraction. Men's desire often leads them to genuinely believe that they love someone, until sex clarifies the situation for them.

A need – love is most definitely not the "need" to be with someone. If you "**need**" someone to fulfill your life, to support you, in order to be happy or whatever, then you have some issues that counseling (or maybe this manual) should be used to help you sort out.

"True" love most definitely involves **wanting** to have the object of your love around you for all time, **but it should NOT be a need!** When you feel you "need" someone in your life, you are not a "whole" person – you are a dependant (dependant on **them**, in order to be happy, whole or whatever) and that is unfair on him or her, **and** you. If you enter a relationship on a "need" basis, it also means that losing them will be an unnecessarily painful experience.

Conditional – if you find yourself saying (or thinking) that you would love him/her if only... or you would love him/her **more** if... then we're talking more of an ideal than love. There is a controlling element implied here, and that is not a good thing. Perhaps the biggest and most common mistake people can make, is to assume that they can "change" someone, or that the other person will change automatically (they will "settle down" is a commonly misguided statement), once they are in a relationship. It rarely **ever** happens and if the desired change is one that is necessary in order for you to be truly happy with that person, then you have a problem – **especially** after marriage.

True love is all encompassing – (print and read **GiveTrueFriends**).
There **may** be changes after marriage but unfortunately; they are more likely to be for the worse. If he was selfish before he got

married, he will likely be even more selfish **after** the wedding. If he was abusive before he got married, he'll be even more so, after the wedding. If she was demanding before... you got it...

Ownership – The most dangerous concept of all is to confuse love with "ownership." Some people seem to think that if they have given/pledged their "love" to you - then they **own** you. "You are **mine** and if you ever leave me, I will kill you!" "If **I** can't have you, then no one else will!" That is pure **"ownership"** – it has nothing whatsoever, to do with love. This is a major (and dangerous) "control" issue.

On more than one occasion I observed couples who lived together (in one case for 6 years), and then they got married. Within 18 months they were on the divorce route. Why? Because one or both of them treated the marriage certificate as "ownership papers," and they started behaving as we so often do when we "own" something. We don't tend to look after things that we "own," to the degree that we do with things that don't belong to us. I will never understand why married couples who are supposedly "in love," wouldn't **dream** of treating a total **stranger** anywhere **near** as badly as they treat one another. They will **say** things to one another, scream and shout at one another, and be mean to one another in ways that they would **never** behave with a stranger. What **is** that? It sure adds weight to the old saying that "familiarity breeds contempt" but **however** you see it – it certainly is not the behaviour of "true" love.

So What IS Love?
Everyone tends to have their own definition, but for me - love is a wonderfully powerful all-consuming **feeling** – typically, a **warm** feeling that spreads from the heart to the whole of your body.

That feeling creates a strong (sometimes almost overpowering) desire to contribute in every possible way to the other person's happiness - **and that... is... all**! Love is a song in your heart that becomes more beautiful with every day.

That wonderful feeling will **naturally** lead to an intense **desire** to spend as much time as possible with the "producer" of the feeling, but the desire is not love in itself – it is (sometimes), merely a product of love.

I believe you can only experience "true love," when you truly love yourself. If the object of your love fills a hole in your life then you are experiencing a distortion of love that will sometimes seem even more **powerful** than true love, as you convince yourself that you "can't live without them."

What happens, when that object (or person) leaves, or is taken away from you by illness or death? Then the hole seems bigger than ever, and that is where love becomes associated with pain. When something is torn from you (leaving a chasm that "must" be filled), of **course** you are going to feel pain. There is no pain quite like it.

When your love fills a hole in your life, that is when it becomes distorted with feelings of ownership, expectation, jealousy, control, and so on. You will expect that person:

~ To be **where** you want them – **when** you want them there

~ To **behave** the way you want them to

~ To never again look at other people of the opposite sex, and

~ To do what **you** want them to do – **when** you want them to do it.

That is **not** love – it is a terrible distortion of love, and the "pain" of love will certainly be felt in that relationship, as your partner so often "doesn't measure up.

Only when you are a complete person, can you experience true love, because that love will no longer be filling a hole – it will merely enhance what is already a great experience – the experience of your life.

Love is...

~ **Acceptance** – accepting the person for who they are and helping to change only those things that **they** want to change

~ **Freedom** – doing all in your power to set the other person free to be the best that they can be

~ **Caring** – about every aspect of the other person's life, and caring enough to do even those things that you may not really enjoy doing, but which you know will help or please him/her in some way

104

- ~ **Supporting** – lifting them up when they're down, helping to erase those debilitating little fears that create so many obstacles in our lives

- ~ **Wanting the best** for them, and doing whatever you can to help them get it

- ~ **Tolerance and kindness** – even when you may be feeling anything but, at any particular point in time

- ~ **Honesty** – being **truthful** with them even when it's really hard to do so

- ~ **Encouraging** them to be the best – to do those things that they really want to do, but are afraid to begin

You cannot MAKE someone love you

It is not possible to "make" someone love you, or to make yourself love someone else. You are either compatible at that level or you aren't. Often you will wonder what is wrong with you when you realise that a person who obviously loves you, is a truly wonderful person - yet you have no feeling for him or her at all. It's just the way life is.

It **is** quite possible however, to **learn** to love someone - but if the object of your love appears to have no interest in you, then you are best to save yourself a lot of heartache, by moving on as quickly as possible.

Where does it start?

Love may start the minute you meet someone, or it may take years to develop. The first thing you may feel is...

- ~ You like them and they interest you

- ~ You want to spend more time in their company – you want to see them again

- ~ You will notice that you think about them a lot – even when you're doing other things

- ~ You'll notice that just thinking about them, brings a smile to your face, and soon

- ~ That smile will spread to your heart - making you feel warm at the same time.

~ You will find that you want to spend more and more time with the person

~ While you are with them – nothing else matters

~ When a call or an email comes through that you believe is from that person, you will feel your heart start to race, and you may breathe faster

~ If you hear that they're not well – you will feel a tremendous anxiety, and will want to drop everything to be with them

~ You think more about what you can do for **them** than what they can do for **you**

~ You start being more concerned for their welfare than you are for your own, and this is where the distortion can begin again if you're not careful. You must never fall into the trap of not taking care of yourself

~ Especially though – you want to contribute to their happiness more than anything else in the world, and doing so makes **you** happier, than anything you can think of.

Love is not affected by age, looks, education, wallet, or intellect. You love them for "who they are," and **nothing else matters**.

Some friends in the US whom I love dearly, asked if I would "want to come down and see if I could help them with their relationship," which was about to end after more than 25 years. I said "Would I **want** to come down – **NO WAY** – what person in their right mind would **want** to get between two good friends in one of the most sensitive times of their life?" But then I said "**Will** I come down? Of **course** I will – because that's what friends do."

This was a traumatic time for my own family because I was still recovering from an illness that had come extremely close to taking my life, and my specialist strongly opposed flying, because he had no way of knowing if I would survive the trip.

Hearing that prognosis, my wife was adamant that I should not go but then my **13-year-old daughter** said, "Mum – I know Dad is not going to take any silly chances and they are **such** good people. They need him more than we do right now, and I know they'll take good

106

care of him." They did, and I did survive albeit with one scary day, but that (to me) was true love on behalf of all parties.

Print and read "**WhatWouldYouDieFor**"

Love is absolutely **not** about doing the things for the other person that you love doing anyway – it's doing the things that you **hate** doing – but doing them anyway - **because** you love that person. My wife used to get really angry when I exhibited all the enthusiasm of a herd of plankton heading down a whale's throat, over being asked to pick her up from work (I **loathe** driving in end-of-work traffic), but as I so often pointed out to her – I always **did** (pick her up).

If I didn't love her I would have happily told her to catch a bus "cos I don't drive at that time of the day."

I am not a keen renovator (to put it mildly) but I have done a **huge** amount of renovation on our house, because it makes my wife so happy as she sees the improvements. **That** is love. "True" love is selfless, and devoid of any semblance of control.

"Feeling" questions

Some useful questions to ask before trying to evaluate your feelings as love (or not), or (especially) before making any **commitment** to love include...

~ If absolutely **nothing** changed about this person – would you still want to spend the rest of your life with him or her? Remember - possibly the single - biggest mistake that people can make in choosing a partner, is thinking they will be able to change them.

~ **Why**? What is it about them that makes you feel that way? Are **you** going to have to make changes in order for this relationship to work? **Any** conditions (whatsoever) applied to a relationship imply, distorted love. Of **course** there will likely be **adjustments** to be made, but you should consider what those adjustments will be, **very** carefully. If they include changing the inherent "you," you need to get on a fast bike and start pedaling.

~ Is this a person that you have a lot of respect for? You can live with a person that you don't love, but just try living with a person that you don't respect. Only a saint will do that successfully.

~ How does this person make you feel when you are together? Words like "Great / Wonderful / Fantastic..." are meaningless –

a good fart can make you feel like that. The words that you should look for are "I feel stronger, more free..." and so on.

RELATIONSHIPS

Love is NOT enough – (hopefully) you will meet many people in this world that you will "love to bits" but you may find that you couldn't **live** with them, if your life depended on it.

Commitment questions

Vitally important questions to ask before committing to a long-term relationship (or marriage) include...

~   Are we compatible with regard to religion?

~   If not, what challenges is that likely to create?

~   Do we **both** want children?

~   Do we both want the same **number** of children?

~   Do our ideas on **raising** children match...

   *   What is acceptable versus unacceptable **behaviour** from children?
   *   How much **time** should be spent with children What is acceptable **punishment** for poor behaviour?
   *   What (if any) **religion** will they be aligned with?
   *   What **schooling** do you want for them?
   *   Do you **vaccinate** or not...)?

~   Have both parties been tested for fertility?

~   If either party turns out to be infertile – what then?

~   Does either partner have a criminal record or was either person charged for an offence at any time – in these crazy times I don't consider it at **all** over the top to ask them to provide a Police background check?

~   What kind of an upbringing did each partner have?

~   What are the likely impacts of that upbringing on the relationship?

~   Has this person faced any serious trauma in their lifetime?

108

- If so, how sure can you be that it has been dealt with?
- Is there any past relationship that either partner needs to know about?
- Is either party jealous by nature?
- Is either party possessive by nature? (This is one to watch – it can be dangerous).
- How does your proposed partner deal with anger (do they get physical e.g. - or do they get drunk)?
- Are both parties romantic?
- Is romance important to us?
- Do we agree on what makes a romantic evening?
- Do we share enough interests not to get bored with one another?
- Do our views on tidiness match?
- If not – what compromises will be acceptable to both parties?
- Are both willing to help with chores and cooking?
- Is either one of you wanting to go back to school for any reason?
- If so, is the other prepared to support you until you graduate?
- Is either party a "perfectionist?"
- Do you agree on pets?
- What annoyingly "bad habits" does your proposed partner have (e.g. not putting the lid on the toothpaste, tossing dirty clothes into a corner rather than in the washing bin, not cleaning up after him/herself...?
- Is this likely to be an issue?
- What are the things that bug your proposed partner most in life? This will tell you a lot about them and be a big help in deciding compatibility (or not)?
- Do you see any signs of mental, sexual, or physical abusiveness in the other person?
- Do they have control issues?
- Are you agreed on both partners working?

- Do your views on either party **not** working match?
- Are your sexual appetites compatible?
- Does your intended partner have any unusual sexual preferences that we should know about?
- If either party is sexually experienced and active – have they had a check-up recently (for aids e.g.)?
- Has either party ever had herpes or any other STD (sexually Transmitted Disease)?
- Are you **physically** compatible (do you **both** like lots of hugs etc.)?
- What are their expectations of you?
- What are your expectations of them?
- Are they a party person, an outdoor person, or a homebody?
- What about you?
- Do we agree on money – saving/spending/investing?
- Is your intended partner a sports fanatic (watching or playing)?
- What does that mean with regard to your relationship?
- Does he or she drink alcohol and if so – how much/how regularly?
- Is he/she a recovering alcoholic?
- Are your views on drugs shared by your proposed partner?
- Has he/she ever taken drugs?
- If so, what were the circumstances around that?
- Does he or she gamble and if so – what form does that take?
- Is there a history of alcoholism, drug taking, or gambling in the family?
- How do both parties feel about drug taking (including marijuana)?
- Are there any debilitating illnesses in the family (Alzheimer's, Parkinson's, etc)

~ If so – do you know what that means for you and are you willing to accept that responsibility?

~ Do you both agree on the amount of time you would like to spend together (in each other's company in other words)?

~ Are you agreed on how that time should be spent (e.g. walking, dining out, movies out (or in the home) or just listening to music while snuggled up on a couch...)?

~ Do both parties get along with the in-laws?

~ And so on

In the real world, things like money, beliefs, misaligned expectations, family, long-term goals, views on having/raising kids and so on, can be total deal-breakers. Love does **not** imply compatibility, in any way.

External forces have a huge impact on our lives. To dismiss them is to be naive. While love can definitely **help** you get through many things, on its own – it is not enough. If a proposed partner is into alcohol or drugs, you need to **really** take a step back and consider seriously if this is a relationship that should continue, or should you be running in the opposite direction. If there is a likelihood of a disabling illness (Parkinsons, Alzheimers, early arthritis, MS...) are you ready to spend the rest of your life taking care of him/her? In this regard, it is **so** easy to succumb to doing that which appears to be "right" by not letting the problem stop you from going ahead. But if there is a possibility that you will end up hating the person (and yourself) years later, for the prison you then find yourself in – who do you think you really helped?

Best friends – another misguided concept is that your partner should be your best friend – why? Best friends are the people that you complain to, when your partner "pisses you off" about something. It's important to have other people in your life besides your partner so that you don't become stifled by your relationship. When you make your partner your best friend, they eventually become your whole life, and once again, dependence begins to enter the scene.

The ultimate freedom

True love sets you, and the object of your love free, in a way that nothing else can. Remember the favourite "life" compliment mentioned earlier from my wife?

Her expansion of her life is the thing that gives me the greatest pleasure, and I have always told her that if she finds someone else that she feels she would be happier with, then that's where she should be. If she discovered that the "grass wasn't greener" and wanted to return (assuming that I hadn't moved on too), my only condition would be that she be sure that that was where she really **wanted** to be (and that she didn't bring anything back with her [e.g. An STD or a pregnancy]). My one goal in our partnership is to help her to be the best that she **can** be, in whatever she wants to do.

In real love, you should always want the very best for your partner, but **not at the cost of your own happiness**. I would be happy to see her go **only**, if I believed she was going to be happier in her new environment. My own sadness would be short lived because in the first instance, I would always have the memories, in the second instance – I would be happy knowing that **she** was happy, and third – I know there would be someone else that I would love just as much (but differently), waiting for me to knock on her door.

In summary – what is love? Best ask the kids...

Since forever, people have searched for the meaning of love but even the great philosophers with their profound definitions, could not fully touch its true essence. In a survey of 4-8 year olds, kids shared their views on love.

~ "Love is that first feeling you feel before all the bad stuff gets in the way."

~ "When my grandmother got arthritis, she couldn't bend over and paint her toenails anymore. So my grandfather does it for her all the time, even when his hands got arthritis too. That's love."

~ "When someone loves you, the way she says your name is different. You know that your name is safe in her mouth."

~ "Love is when a girl puts on perfume and a boy puts on shaving cologne and they go out and smell each other."

112

~ "Love is when you go out to eat and give somebody most of your French fries without making them give you any of theirs."

~ "Love is when someone hurts you. And you get so mad but you don't yell at him because you know it would hurt his feelings."

~ "Love is what makes you smile when you're tired."

~ "Love is when my mommy makes coffee for my daddy and she takes a sip before giving it to him, to make sure the taste is OK and it's not too hot."

~ "Love is when you kiss all the time. Then when you get tired of kissing, you still want to be together and you talk more. My mommy and daddy are like that. They look gross when they kiss but they look happy, and sometimes they dance in the kitchen while kissing."

~ "Love is what's in the room with you at Christmas if you stop opening presents and listen."

~ "If you want to learn to love better, you should start with a friend who you hate."

~ "When you tell someone something bad about yourself and you're scared she won't love you anymore. But then you get surprised because not only does she still love you, she loves you even more."

~ "There are 2 kinds of love. Our love and God's love. But God makes both kinds of them."

~ "Love is when you tell a guy you like his shirt, then he wears it every day."

~ "Love is like a little old woman and a little old man who are still friends even after they know each other so well."

~ "Love happened at my piano recital, I was on a stage and scared. I looked at all the people watching me and saw my daddy waving and smiling. He was the only one doing that. I wasn't scared anymore."

~ "My mommy loves me more than anybody. You don't see anyone else kissing me to sleep at night."

~ "Love is when mommy gives daddy the best piece of chicken."

~ "Love is when mommy sees daddy smelly and sweaty and still says he is handsomer than Robert Redbird."

~ "Love is when your puppy licks your face even after you left him alone all day."

~ "Love goes on even when you stop breathing and you pick up where you left off when you reach heaven."

~ "I know my older sister loves me because she gives me all her old clothes and has to go out and buy new ones."

~ "You really shouldn't say 'I love you' unless you mean it. But if you mean it, you should say it a lot. People forget and need to be told."

~ "I let my big sister pick on me because my Mom says she only picks on me because she loves me. So I pick on my baby sister because I love her."

~ "Love cards like Valentine's cards say stuff on them that we'd like to say ourselves, but we wouldn't be caught dead saying."

~ "When you love somebody, your eyelashes go up and down and little stars come out of you."

~ "Love means you never have to be lonely. There's always somebody to love, even if it's just a squirrel or a kitten."

~ "You can break love, but it won't die."

What more can anyone say?

How do you find love?

Everyone has his or her own ideas about this, but the wonderful thing about our "age of communication" is that we are no longer limited to "what's in the village." With affordable travel available to most, with confidential introduction agencies and the internet especially, you may find your partner anywhere in the world. I found mine in the Philippines (not via the internet albeit), but my sister found her partner in England - via the internet, while living in Australia.

One thing is for **certain** and that is... there absolutely is **someone** waiting out there for you and in order to **find** love (or to be found **by** love) **you have to be available!!**

Need versus want

When I moved to Canada I hoped with all my heart that my wife would follow, but I never **expected** that she would. She doesn't "need" me in her life - any more than I need her, and when people asked, "Doesn't that scare you?" my honest answer was, "No..." it changes the whole concept of being together. Because she doesn't need me, I never expect that she will come home on any given day. I **anticipate** that she will, and when she does – I know it's because she **wants** to be there. It's wonderful!

The worst thing in the event that she did **not** follow me from New Zealand would have been eleven years of wonderful memories, followed by the excitement of what the future might bring.

By my calculations at that time there were approximately six billion people in the world, and my understanding is that on a world basis – women slightly outnumber men (hey this is **my** story ok). So, assuming that women made up let's say 55% of the population - that meant there were approximately 3.3 billion women in the world. Now if only 10% of those women were in an age group that might be interested in me – that left 330,000,000, and let's say only 30% of them were "available" – leaving 99,000,000. Now if only **1%** of those available women would actually be **interested** in me – that meant there were **1,089,000** women waiting for me to call - and how could I be sad about that?

After my Mum got over her separation, she longed for a **real** partner – someone she could talk to, a "shoulder to cry on," and a companion to share the rest of her life with. Of course she never found such a person - because she never **went** anywhere, where love could find **her**!

If you're a homebody then agencies or the Internet are possibly the best places for you to start. Otherwise, join singles groups, join Rotary or the Lions or Lionesses clubs, join Toastmasters, do community or charity work – whatever works for you, but **do** "get out."

Think about the **type** of person that you would like to meet and go to the places that such a person might be found. If you are not a sporting type or a nightclub person then **don't go looking there,** because the chances of meeting a **compatible** mate in those places will be very slim. You'll end up being a "golf widow" or whatever.

It really pays to have at least **some** idea of a plan, and the worst thing that is likely to happen (assuming that you approach this sensibly), is that you may end up having some real fun – getting out and doing different things in your life.

Print and read **Red Roses**

What is love?
Love is the highest level of (unconditional) affection that you can experience, (for another person, life, this beautiful planet, an animal etc.)

How do you know when you are "in love?" (with another person e.g.)

~ Just the **thought** of that person, brings a smile to both your heart **and** your face

~ Nothing seems to matter anymore – just that they are 'there'

~ Your heart quickens at the thought that a telephone or email message might be from him/her

~ He/she occupies your thoughts constantly

~ Time doesn't exist (except to go ridiculously quickly) when you are together (and slowly when you are not)

~ The only thing that's important when you're apart is when you will see them again, and

~ Much much more – but **most** importantly...

~ You want the world **for** them, but need nothing **from** them – other than their presence.

Whenever you think you are "in love" re-check "what love is not" to be sure.

Love can also create desire - to be with that person for all time because of the pleasure derived from that association and as long as it does not become a 'requirement,' it remains true love. Associated with feelings of love, we often find feelings of respect, admiration, adoration, caring, nurturing and so on, but they are not love in themselves - they can each exist in isolation.

Can love die?
I believe "perceived" love can, but not real love.

In summary
Personal relationships are the most important thing in our lives (next to our health), and the thing we most often screw up.

Know what you want **BEFORE** you enter into **any** relationship of importance. Consider what you are prepared to put **into** the relationship and equally – you need to know what your intended partner expects **from** the relationship.

If the most important part of a partnership for you is watching TV and working around the property together, and **they** want someone to go camping and hiking with – it doesn't matter **how** much you like or are attracted to each other – it **isn't going to work!**

Harmony – it is not possible to create harmony by trying to drag your partner into **your** world – no matter **how** much better you think that world would be for them. Harmony is created by getting into **their** world and when you do, they will be more willing to try a little of yours.

Change – the biggest mistake after entering into a relationship without knowing what you or the other person wants, is going into it with the belief that you can **change** them. If there is something about them that you feel **needs** to change in order for the two of you to be truly happy, then you should run while you can. It almost **never** happens. Growth does **NOT** come from making a person become just like you – it comes from learning how to live with and perhaps eventually love, the differences.

Expectation – the next biggest mistake and perhaps the most common one, is expectation. The surest thing (if not the only thing) that expectation does – is to set you up for disappointment.

Check-it-out – perhaps the three most important words you can add to your vocabulary. Don't **ever** allow yourself to get into the habit of assuming what someone said, what they **meant** by what they said, how they feel, what they're doing, or what they're thinking. In by **far** the majority of situations **you will be wrong!** If it's important **always** "check... it... out!" The worst crime you can commit in a relationship, and the one that will come back on you the hardest, is to wrongfully accuse someone.

Check in – don't wait for an argument to start – **check in** with your partner from time to time to see how you're doing and to tell them what you like or **don't** enjoy about what **they** are doing. You'd be amazed at how many relationships this simple act could save.

And finally – some (if not all) of you may feel that I have gone over the top with all these questions and things. The simple fact is - you **are** going to meet with the answers one way or another, and finding out **after** you've tied the knot – is often **far** too late. It's your call.

You are approximately half way through the program now so print and fill out a copy of the **Personal Evaluation-02.**

When you have finished, open your first copy and compare the forms. If you have been genuinely applying yourself to the manual, you should see some extremely positive changes happening.

When you are satisfied, seal **both** copies back in an envelope to be reviewed at the end of the program (and whenever you feel ready to do another one in the future).

Chapter 11

PROBLEM SOLVING
The purpose of this section is to provide you with a template that will allow you to address and solve almost any problem you may encounter.

~ By the end of the section you'll be able to:

~ List the four steps of the problem solving process, and

~ **Demonstrate** the process in action

The four steps are:
1. Define it
2. Classify it
3. Attack it
4. Solve it

What in fact is a problem?
Try defining that for yourself before reading on.

In the normal sense, I guess you could say that it's anything that we don't have an immediate solution to, and which in some way is important to us.

On the negative side:

~ They may impede our progress

~ They may hinder our achievement

~ They almost **always** cause stress

~ They may affect our health both physically and mentally, as a result of the stress they create

~ They will often affect our relationships with others, and...

~ They can multiply faster than rabbits if allowed to

On the positive side:

~ They can cure boredom

~ They provide excellent learning opportunities, and

How your problems affect you, will depend almost entirely - on **how you ALLOW them to!!!** In other words - your own attitude will be your problem's most powerful ally, or its worst enemy. Only **you** can make the choice!

> How your problems affect you will depend almost entirely, on how you **ALLOW** them to.
>
> *Tom Grbich*

Many problems are real and can be solved in practical terms while perhaps many more, are simply "imagined." Whatever the case, they must be treated with equal importance!

Never forget that if a problem has been "eating you up" then it has real power, and shouldn't be treated lightly no matter how ridiculous it may appear.

A close friend and cherished member of my martial arts school just literally "disappeared" one week. When no one had seen or heard from him for over three weeks, the scouts were sent out. We discovered he'd left his job - his accommodation, and was nowhere to be found.

Eventually one of the guys in the school accidentally met "John" working in a Supermarket. He talked him into at least coming to see me one more time, before dropping out of our lives forever, if that was what he really wanted. So John turned up the following Thursday evening and it didn't take long to realise that a training evening wasn't the place, and nor would it afford the time, to really assist him. I asked him to go home and write down everything - however ridiculous, that was bothering him, and bring the list to my home for discussion on the following evening.

When he arrived the next day having completed his task, he was already looking a little sheepish. "A lot of these things look pretty stupid now," he admitted. My response was to advise that they very likely were, but it was important to remind himself that they'd taken him to the brink of suicide in the past month. It would have been foolish therefore; to treat them with anything less than the respect that something so powerful deserved.

We went through each item with me questioning everything he'd written. By the time we'd finished he was laughing (somewhat hysterically) at himself and shed a few tears, but the problems were no longer with him.

John stayed with the class for another four years then married and settled down with two children. A great Dad, and one who (to the best of my knowledge) has never had his problems take control of him again.

Most problems stem from:
~ A lack of information, knowledge, or experience

~ An overactive imagination

~ A dominant ego, and/or

~ Negative attitudes

So where to from here?

DEFINE IT - find out just what the problem really is. In doing this, it really helps to **WRITE IT DOWN**.

While the problem is inside you, confusion prevails because **you are part of the problem**! You'll 'beat up' on yourself to a greater and greater level, and the problem/s will continue to grow. It's vital that you **separate** yourself from the issue so that you can devote your full attention to **solving** it, rather than **living** it. Just as writing your goals down puts **YOU** in the position of power, so does writing down your problems.

In many instances, the simple act of writing the problem down will see you with an answer. If it doesn't, then you'll at least be in a position to accurately define the source now, and you just can't hope to proceed until you really know what that is. Take a moment to write down any issues that have been bothering you in your day-to-day life, in your "**Things to Work on**" page.

CLASSIFY IT - in terms of importance - is it really worth worrying about? If the answer to this is "Yes", then:

Ask yourself what **makes** it a problem - is it that you can't find a way around it, is it in fact something that you can't do anything about, is it something that **must** be overcome in order for you to go on, or be happy? Are there alternatives?

Once you've classified it you're now in a position to...

ATTACK IT - by creating your own army of information. Gather all the information that you have available to you, and look at it from every possible angle.

There is probably no more important statement in relation to solving any problem - gather every **shred** of information, however irrelevant it may seem at the time - **write it down** if need be, and this will become your assault force, to be used against what will now be a very worried problem.

If your own knowledge is lacking, then seek **more information** - from books, magazines, and friends.

Look to professional help in the form of appropriate courses, consultants, or counselors.

If it is something that you simply can't do anything about - i.e. it is out of your control, or beyond your authority or capabilities, then find someone who does have the power to do it. If this is not possible, then you really have two choices left. Either you walk away from it, or just learn to live with it.

SOLVE IT or dissolve it

You must face the fact that in this imperfect world of ours, we won't always be able to fix things. There's nothing bad about this - nothing to be ashamed of. Sometimes we just have to be prepared to walk away, or train our minds to 'let it be,' and concentrate on the positive things in our lives.

Both of these acts are still **a form** of solution even if not the **ideal** one. The fact still remains, that if the problem is no longer with you, then it is **NO LONGER A PROBLEM.**

Hopefully though, in most situations, having defined the problem, having classified it, and having attacked it to find what you need to do to overcome it, you are now ready to solve it.

What would be the measure of when a problem is solved for you? For me, a problem is solved when it is no longer seen to be an obstacle - when it no longer bothers you.

A practical example follows – read to gather information, try solving it yourself by following the "problem solving process," and then read on:

SITUATION – in one of my roles as a Security Systems Sales Manager, we were required to provide security within a large warehouse, that had birds in it. The traditional methods of protecting an area of this size include:

~ Vibration sensors on the walls to detect someone breaking through

~ Wires that go through metal loops and make an alarm connection in the event that someone leans on them or tries to remove a panel, or an infra-red "fence" using infra red beams around the perimeter so that if anyone makes a hole and climbs through, the beams will be broken and an alarm will result.

We were up against intense competition from more established companies, and we wanted to come up with a cheaper method of providing protection to differentiate ourselves from our competitors.

Unfortunately, the only other detectors suitable for protecting this type of building (passive infra red detectors) can be activated by birds. If we were to use those detectors therefore, we would almost **certainly** experience false alarms, and security would be impaired by the "cry wolf" syndrome.

DEFINE THE PROBLEM
How would **you** define this problem?

Our problem was to find a way of making those detectors work without risking false alarms.

CLASSIFY IT - was it important? Yes it was.

Why was it a problem? It was a problem because the area simply

had to be secured, and as a lesser known company at the time, we needed something to gain more recognition from the business community.

Alternatives - were there alternatives? Yes there were. Unfortunately the alternatives were expensive and our competition would almost certainly be taking that route.

ATTACK IT - **always** look at the alternatives first - in this case there were alternatives as mentioned, but they didn't help us in this situation.

GATHER INFORMATION - to better understand the problem, let's look at how the passive infrared detector works. The detector sees its world in terms of temperature, looking for rapid **changes** and/or **movements** of temperature, within its zones of observation. In other words, if I placed you in the middle of a room which was covered by one of these detectors and you didn't move, you would be deemed to be part of the environment and there would be no alarm.

If I then set your trousers or skirt on fire however, the rapid change in temperature would almost certainly trigger an alarm.

The other thing that would cause an alarm is if you moved. The detector knows that objects are not **supposed** to move so if your temperature moved to another of its zones of detection then it would be pretty convinced that this should be an alarm situation.

Now let's consider the **prime requirement** of the infrared detector in this role. Its prime requirement ideally, is to detect the presence of **intruders** (people) to the exclusion of all else.

What is **OUR** prime requirement in this situation? Our prime requirement is to find a way to overcome the problem of potential false alarms, **without compromising the level of security**, and thereby allow the detectors to fulfill **their** prime requirement.

What is DIFFERENT?

Our next move is to look for differences between that which we **do** want to detect, versus that which we do **not**. When we compare birds to human beings, we find the most potentially useful differences to be in...

~ Size – birds (thank goodness) tend to be a lot smaller than humans, and

~ A bird's body temperature is considerably higher that a human's. It is important to note however, that the insulation provided by the bird's feathers tends to overcome the heat factor.

These two features would suggest that a bird would have to be a lot closer to the detector before being noticed, than a man would be.

So keeping the birds at a distance from the detectors would appear to be a solution in part, but how do we achieve this?

More information is required - let's take a look at the nature of a bird's activity in such an environment. We find here that there are two main factors affecting the activity of birds in a building... *light, and perching facilities.*

THE SOLUTION. From the information gained by following the above steps, it seems to stand to reason that if we place our detectors away from windows as the main source of light, and spoil any potential perches nearby, then we will have markedly improved the problem.

Note that we have only **IMPROVED,** not **REMOVED,** the problem. Is there anything else that we can do?

BACK TO OUR INFORMATION
Looking at our information and questioning why this solution is only a partial one, we have to accept that the measures taken will never provide a 100% guarantee that no bird will ever fly close enough to any one detector to trigger it.

Just read that again... "any **ONE** detector." There lies our answer - we can't stop them from approaching any **individual** detector, but we can certainly position two detectors, in such a way that a bird cannot activate both at the same time. By wiring them so that both must activate in order to cause an alarm, the problem is solved. Small things again?

Every class I have ever run has always solved this problem even though they knew nothing about security – simply by following the Process.

The interesting thing though, is how quickly people move to trying to **beat** the process, by attempting to solve the problem right away. Again this is a problem of our education system - the first person with the answer is the "smartest," and they get all the attention. Interestingly - in my experience, Sales People as a group have always made the most attempts to solve the problem without completing the process.

Thirty two failed attempts to solve the problem without completing the process is the highest that I have experienced and as frustrating as it was for them, they did finally solve the problem - by following the process.

The least number of attempts to bypass the system and solve the problem was 7.

Exercise:

Go back to some of the issues that you wrote on your 'Things to Work on' page, and apply this process to resolving them. And remember – if you struggle to come up with an answer, it's only because you haven't got enough information (or possibly the **right**) information.

Chapter 12

ATTITUDE

The purpose of this section is to provide you with an understanding of how much of what you perceive to be "good" or "bad" / "positive" or "negative" in your lives, may have been (and may still be being), caused by your own attitude.

By the end of this chapter you will be able to:

~ Describe how to control your responses to events around you.

~ Describe those "attitudes" that lead to "positivity" in your life

~ Describe those "attitudes" that lead to "negativity" in your life

~ Relate how "attitude" can be in total **control** of your life, and

~ Describe how you're going to take that control back

Is your attitude impressing the kind of people who can REALLY help your future?

If this sounds somewhat similar to "Ego" – you're right.   Ego and Attitude tend to go hand-in-hand.

From the moment of our birth, repetition in certain areas begins to condition what we think and believe.   As we travel through life - having been conditioned to think and act in certain ways, we'll find things that reinforce the behaviour that is now coming out of those "attitudes."   That behaviour will bring results, which, (again determined by our thinking), we will see as "good," "bad," or otherwise.   Go back and review the Behaviour Cycle.

Interestingly, the heads of fifty or so of the top businesses in America were once asked, "If you were allowed to make your hiring decision on only **one** element of a candidate's skills, qualities, or experience, what element would you choose?"   The unanimous reply was "attitude."

You can teach skills to a monkey, and experience comes only with time. A person with the right "attitude" however, will learn those skills in a fraction of the time that another person might take, and he/she will apply him/herself to **gaining** the experience, in a way that will almost always be of benefit to all concerned.

So to change everything in our lives, we first have to change how we **think**. The changes in our actions will follow automatically.

Quote: "If we could kick the person who causes us the most problems in this life, most of us wouldn't be able to sit down for a month." *Originator unknown.*

Print and read "**Attitude**"

In order to understand **ANYTHING** it helps to know what we're talking about. So what does this word actually mean? An attitude effectively, is a "position," a state of mind or feeling, which is taken or derives in response, to something else.

Basically, attitudes are the way in which we **CHOOSE** to see things. This is fundamentally the most important thing for you to understand and accept. Our attitude is **NOT** something that is forced upon us, and it is **not** inherited. We often **ADOPT** the attitudes of our parents, families or peers, but adopting is something you **DO** - it is not something that just **IS** (thank goodness). In essence, attitudes are our personal philosophies - formed by prejudices, environment, upbringing, and especially; experiences.

Attitudes affect - or are affected **BY** three main factors - physical, mental, & emotional; broadly manifesting themselves in actions that will be seen as either positive or negative by those around you.

Positive attitudes are those that are seen to be **con**structive while negative attitudes tend to be **de**structive. Positive attitudes come from what...? Open thinking, a desire to learn, feeling good about yourself and your environment, and knowing that you're in control of your life (for example).

Where do negative attitudes tend to come from? Fear, insecurity, and more than anything else that I can think of - low self-image.

Go to your **Personal Discoveries** page and take a few minutes to write down one or two of your attitudes that you would put in the **positive** column, and any that you can think of that belong the **negative** column.

If you're physically run down you'll find it harder and harder to maintain a positive attitude.

If your thinking is unhealthy (poor self-image egg.) your attitudes will drift to the negative, and if you're in an emotional state, once again your attitudes will very likely be negative. Foods and chemicals can also affect your attitude so you can **see the importance of looking after your whole being,** if you want to be truly positive most, if not all of the time.

To change your attitudes, often all that is needed is an open mind, a desire for things to be different in your life, the will to make it happen, and more information.

Who is in charge?
I spoke a while ago about attitudes being the way in which you **choose** to perceive things. It's important to understand at this point that other people's attitudes or actions - are **nothing to do with you**. You **CANNOT**, be affected by the actions of others unless you **choose** to be!

Other people will provide you with lots of **opportunities** to be upset, to be unhappy, to be angry, and/or to be happy, enthusiastic, motivated, etc. Go to your **Personal Discoveries** page again and write down any examples of opportunities you can think of, that **you** have bought into. Which ones do you tend to buy into most **readily** (positive or negative)? Why is that do you think (maybe another look at your "needs" chart would help here)?

What you **do** with those opportunities is entirely up to you! If I saw you at a restaurant and for some mildly unusual reason I chose to go over and throw up in your lap, I'd have just given you two powerful opportunities. One would be to let the situation control you, and the other would be to take control of the situation

The opportunity **most** people would run with is to let the situation control them - allow me to ruin their evening - giving me tremendous power over them in the process. You could burst into tears, fly into a rage and perhaps even bust me one, **OR** - you could excuse yourself, go and get cleaned up, and refuse to allow a scum-bucket like me to affect your outing. I'm not suggesting that any of these responses is wrong. All I am asking is - who was in charge of the particular response that you went with?

It's important to appreciate that the initial reactions / responses are almost impossible to eliminate. It's how soon **after** that initial response / reaction that you're able to take charge, that is the real measure of where you're "at" in your life. Like any habit - initially you'll reach for the light switch but you'll then consciously decide, not to turn it on.

Eventually you'll be so "with it," that the natural move to the light switch will be caught so early in the piece, that it will be imperceptible to anyone around you.

In our restaurant situation you may **still** choose to bust me, but now you'll have made a conscious decision that that is what is:

a) Going to give you the greatest satisfaction, and/or

b) Be the best lesson to me.

Picture yourself in the above situation where you react normally/instinctively to your attitude. You leap up and bust me a good one and I drop dead with a stroke from the shock of your blow. And then you find that I had no idea of what I was doing because some idiot had spiked my drink. What will your attitude be now?

What is your attitude towards the parent of some little children who are yelling and screaming, running around - uncontrollably hitting each other and other people? How would your attitude change if you found out they had just watched their mother die in a critical care unit, after a month long battle with cancer?

Our attitudes tend to make us incredibly judgmental of other people, and situations around us. The rule should always be - if it bothers you enough – check-it-out - then **choose** your response or reaction - don't be controlled by it!

I strongly recommend that you write those words in your action plan - "check-it-out." The damage we do to ourselves, our relationships, and other people simply because we are too damned lazy to perform this unbelievably simple task is criminal!

My wife is a stickler for tidiness and if there is one thing guaranteed to set her off, it's coming home to an untidy house. Knowing this I would usually do a quick check to make sure things were ok just before she came home (I work from a home office). I had done this one afternoon and returned to my office when suddenly I heard bellowing from the living room.

I went to "check it out" and found that she had called our 5-year-old daughter in and was screaming at her about a Barbie doll's legs sticking out from under the curtain. She was given a damning lecture, along with threats to make her collect **all** her dolls and throw them in the rubbish bin etc. I waited till the sobbing kid ran back to her room with the doll tucked under her arm, and asked how hard it would have been, and how long it would have taken, to "check-it-out" – to ask if our daughter had been the one to leave it there, **before** descending into the tirade?

She went on the defensive with "Well it's **her** doll, and she's **always** leaving them lying around..." I agreed on both counts, but was able to advise her that on this occasion our son had been playing with his toy soldiers – using the Barbie doll as a target. He had "blasted" the doll and tossed it across the room as part of the "explosion," and it had landed under the curtain – just as she had found it. So we now had an extremely distressed little girl who probably was struggling to find anything nice in her heart with regard to her mother, and all for what? Is it any wonder that so many children grow up resenting their parents so bitterly?

It was incredibly interesting for me much later in life, when I looked back at my own childhood. I found that of all the beatings I had received, only one could I remember in acute detail, and that was the one where I had done nothing wrong. Although the intensity of all of the other beatings bore little relationship to the "crime," at least I knew I had done something wrong.

There is nothing quite so damaging as to be punished for a crime for which you are not guilty, so paste those words "check-it-out" on the inside of your forehead and acknowledge them before **any** accusation.

How many times have you gone to a friend or family member who was going through a tough patch? With your understanding of needs, you've given them an opportunity to get away from it all - clear their thinking, by going to a movie, a beach, or whatever, and what was their response. "Oh no, I don't think I'm up to it at the moment."

Strangely, their attitude seems to be that they either deserve to be feeling the way they are and perhaps haven't suffered enough yet, or that their situation is just "too complex" and they can't be helped.

Maybe it's all the attention they're getting? Who knows but it **is** their choice, and typically, no amount of coaxing will get them to change. The trouble is; if you stay down too long, you might forget how to get back up again.

Anyone who has lived on a farm will know that if a cow or a horse goes down and you can't get it on its feet again within a certain period of time, chances are excellent that you never will. There often will be nothing physically wrong with it, yet it will still die because its thinking has become confused. It thinks that when it goes down it's supposed to stay that way by the laws of nature or something.

People don't typically die **physically** from being down too long, but they often die **emotionally**.

If you can't control your responses then quite simply - you are **NOT** in control of your **LIFE**!! If you want to be in control of your life then you simply **MUST**, learn to control your attitudes.

Let's look at how your attitudes affect you:

Our attitudes affect our moods, our emotions, our relations with other people, and of course - our work.

Negative attitudes will make your company unpleasant so people will eventually **avoid** you. They affect your work so ultimately, you may **lose your job**. They affect your "aura" so that people and...

132

prospective employers will be **turned off you**. They make you depressed and unhappy, and this becomes a huge cycle that gets harder and harder to get off.

Most importantly though is the affect that they have on your health.

When asked, "What is the most important thing in our life," we can come up with a host of things – our family, our children, our partner, our Mum and Dad... the list goes on. And how do we "show" those people that they are so important to us? We are "there" for them any time – night or day, we do things for them, we buy them gifts... the list goes on again. The **real** question though, is "How do you do that when you are bed-ridden with illness?"

> **Nothing** in this world is more important than your health – absolutely **nothing**.
>
> *Tom Grbich*

The reality is – you are no use to **anyone** if you have given up your health – you can't "be there" for **anybody** any longer, (including yourself), you can't "do" things for them any longer, and so it goes. **Always** remember – when the oxygen masks fall in an aeroplane – whose do you put on first? You got it – yours. And why is that? Because you can't help your family get theirs on, if you are unconscious can you? And so it is with all of life.

Take a good look at yourself and your achievements to date, and ask yourself "Where have your attitudes contributed to your success, where might they have contributed more, and where have they in fact done little more than to stand in your way. Our attitudes not only control our lives; they ultimately control our destiny. So if you want that life to be a good life – make sure your attitudes are positive ones.

By way of example, let me tell you of a situation that I found myself in. I'd been working for a small security alarm company for just over a year when it was bought out by a much larger company. They had previously specialised in all other aspects of security, except electronic security. My role was Regional Sales Manager at the time and although my new boss had been appointed at the same time as me, he wasn't due to take up the position for a further three months, as he had entered in an ocean-going sailing competition. This meant that I had to set the new division up with the help of one of the other Managers, who had been with the company for many years.

By the time my boss actually started, things were already going well and his peers (who were a truly great bunch of people), began to tease him. They suggested that they were unsure as to why the company had hired him at all when the division was already going so well, and that he would have to watch me or I might take his job. Unfortunately he didn't have much of a sense of humour and took the jibes seriously, gradually making my life more and more difficult.

Then, towards the end of the first year, an audit was carried out on all of the company's divisions. Talking to the auditors I was pleased to find that they had found our operation to be a dream by comparison with most other divisions of the company, but my boss didn't see it that way unfortunately.

I was talking to my Office Manager (let's call her Karen) when he came in and gave us a bit of a dressing down about the fact that we had not cancelled the security guard's license, of a person that I had had to fire.

After he left, I asked Karen to see to it just as soon as she could, but pointed out that it was not that important. A month or so later, she and I were discussing the incredible achievement of the past twelve months. We had been budgeted to make a 30% loss owing to the costs of setting up the new division, but in fact we'd achieved a 16% profit. On top of that, she pointed out that in our twelve months we had installed just under three times the number of alarm systems that the previous company had achieved in the previous twelve months. And we did it with one person less than they had had.

We were in the midst of a self-congratulatory session when our boss came stomping in looking like a thundercloud. Apparently Karen had still not cancelled the security guard's license - and did we get a roasting this time. Wow! He left with her in tears and not a word of thanks for the great year that we had turned in. Karen muttered "The ba....d" as he disappeared around the corner and then turned to see me smiling at her.

"How on earth can you sit there like that after what that 'creature' just did?" she asked. "Karen," I said, "if you think I'm going to let a gross little pimple like him take away the joy and satisfaction of the results we've worked so hard for over the past year, then you really don't know me."

Yes I could have done as many people probably would - jumped up and thumped the table, yelled back at him, and probably told him to shove his job just where it felt worst - but what would that really have achieved? He would have won in every way. Firstly he would have got the reaction that he so obviously wanted, and then he would have had me out of his life. The staff would have lost, I would have lost, and my family would have lost because I didn't have a job to immediately transfer to. Are **YOU** going to let someone like that have power over you? I certainly hope not!

Quote: "No one can make you feel inferior, without your consent." - Originator unknown.

I'm not suggesting that all of this is easy. When you've spent a lifetime allowing yourself to be controlled by your environment, your attitude, and other people, it takes a real effort to break out of it. We talked earlier of "patterns" - about how you walk into a bedroom for example and switch the light on even though it's daytime. You normally go into the bedroom at night-time, and the darkness has conditioned you to turn the light on so you still do it even when it may not in fact be needed. Of greater concern is - how often do you react to situations or **people**, in a manner that not only may not be needed, but is probably not appropriate?

ABSOLUTELY NOTHING GREAT CAN BE ACHIEVED IN THIS LIFE, UNLESS WE ADOPT A POSITIVE ATTITUDE!

In order to effect any lasting improvement in this life, you can almost guarantee that the first change will have to be - a change in attitude.

To hell with ego
One of the most complicated and powerful obstacles to the changing of attitudes, would have to be imagined pride (ego). It is important to separate these two so that we don't create opportunities for more confusion.

Pride I have no problem with. **Real** pride comes from feeling good about yourself, knowing that you are a good person, the satisfaction of doing a good job, doing the right thing by others and so on. Pride comes from **good** things, and projects itself in a good way. Genuine pride is an admirable quality that is seen and respected as such by others. It comes entirely from within - it's an internal thing.

Ego is false pride. Like fools gold it's easy to mistake it for the real thing but it has no value whatsoever, in reality. Ego is the attempt to appear proud, when there really isn't much to be proud of. Pride is a natural thing that tends to sit in the background. It doesn't need reinforcing or external massaging because it's **real**.

Ego is unnatural. It needs constant massaging; it's forever trying to prove itself, and it tries to force itself on other people all the time.

Ego can never be satisfied as it continues to search **ex**ternally, for the satisfaction that can only come, with genuine heartfelt (**in**ternal) pride. In fact ego has probably caused more pain and sorrow in the history of our existence, than any other three human traits put together.

Think of the wars that have been fought over some fool's dented ego. How many wives were left to fend for themselves and their children in the harsh wilderness of America, because some jerk husband's ego forced him to draw a gun against some person that he knew he couldn't beat in a hundred lifetimes? You see the ego is incapable of considering other people; it is self-obsessed.

Having isolated the areas in which attitudes have held you back, it is imperative that you check and see if ego hasn't been the real culprit. Poor attitudes are all too often a symptom of a fragile ego.

In order to overcome the negative effects of ego, it helps first to look at what it is costing you. You should then measure that against what you're gaining from your resulting actions, and you'll usually find an imbalance so great that it will embarrass you.

Questions such as "Is it **REALLY** worth it?" and "What does it **REALLY** matter?" will usually set you on the right path and with a little time and a few reminders, you will never look back.

Surround yourself with positive people.

We are energetic beings and all energy is affected by all other energy. Place a hot iron in a cold tub and the solution in the tub will soon bring the temperature down even as the iron has its own effect.

Everything is relative. If the amount of solution in the tub is small in relation to the size of the iron then the temperature of the solution will be raised far more than the heat of the iron is lowered, and vice versa.

What I am saying is that if you surround yourself for long enough with enough negative people, they will eventually knock the heat out of you. That is unless you have some pretty effective techniques for dealing with it.

If you have someone constantly chipping away at home, work, or wherever you spend a lot of your time, that too will eventually bring you down if you don't have enough positive people in your life, to hold you up. If you can't change their negativity then in your own interests you may just have to leave. It can be a tough decision but it may be one you have to make. My personal belief is that one right everyone should claim in this world - is the right to happiness. And just **no one**, should be allowed to take that from you.

> The one right that **everyone on earth should claim** – is the right to be happy.
>
> *Tom Grbich*

If you print and fill out "**Attitudes Working For You**," you will notice some very direct questions that need to be answered as follows:

~ Is it really **necessary** for the situation to be as it is right now? If there is tension or aggression in the air; people are obviously uncomfortable – what is going on here? Does it **really** need to be this way?

~ If your answer is "Yes," then I hope you will have considered "why?" Are you seeing this situation as it **is,** or as you **are** (what "information" are you working with in other words or; how are you **interpreting** that information)?

If your answer Is "No" then you really do need to take a step back and consider a major change in direction. "Why are you continuing" or "Why **would** you continue" are appropriate questions to have in mind right now.

~ Is ego playing a role here? Chances are absolutely **excellent** that it is. In almost **every** situation of conflict, ego will be in the background throwing fuel on the fire. If that is the case then...

~ How is it **helping** the situation (I can't help but laugh at this question – the ego **never** helps **any** situation)?

Once you have dealt with those questions honestly, it helps a lot to just take a look at what you stand to **gain** from your chosen attitude, and what you stand to **lose** by it. It will help tremendously in guiding a positive course of action from here.

The simple question (which actually can be asked at any point in this process) – "Is this really worth it," will often help you see sense right away and of course you must then decide on how you plan to continue.

EXERCISE:
Add any other "attitudes" that you feel need to be on the list we started earlier.

Go to your **Draft Action Plan** and note what you're going to do to correct your negative attitudes and make sure you continue the positive ones, then...

Note how you see this change benefiting you, and the people around you?

Chapter 13

ENTHUSIASM

The purpose of this chapter is to provide you with the tools to be as enthusiastic as you **want** to be – for as much of the **time** as you would like to be that way.

On completion, you will be able to:

~   Describe what enthusiasm is for you

~   Describe what gets **you** enthusiastic, and

~   Relate how you plan to **be** enthusiastic (or "motivated,") just as much of the time as you want

True enthusiasm comes from the heart.

Enthusiasm (for me) is "Passion with Purpose" and it makes itself known by a feeling of irrepressible joy that almost **has** to be shared - it's too great to keep to myself. What about you? Write your thoughts down in your **Personal Discoveries** page.

Print and read "**Unstoppable**"

Some people wonder if others are "born" enthusiastic. Certainly it would appear that some people are, but I truly believe you can learn to be that way. In my own case I was told that I was born **useless** and it's hard to be enthusiastic about that. Clearly **I** wasn't born enthusiastic but I have taught myself to be that way.

My son I think, **might** have been born enthusiastic. On our first Christmas in Canada as a family, he had got himself seriously grounded. At the age of 6, he had had all of his presents removed one by one from under the Christmas tree, and was washing and drying the dishes on his own for the whole month.

One night a couple of days before Christmas, he was standing on his little blue box so he could reach into the sink, singing away as he washed the dishes. My wife looked at him and said "Jaron – you **do** know you're being punished don't you?" He said "Yeah." So my wife asked "So why are you singing then?" He paused for a moment to look at her and then he replied, "Well you might as well be happy!" A lot of adults could learn from him.

Where does **your** enthusiasm come from? Mine (primarily) comes from...

~ Being the **best I can** be, in everything I do

~ **Enjoying** what I do, and the progress that I see myself making each day

~ **Learning** opportunities

~ Being around **good people**

~ Ensuring I always maintain a **clear conscience**, and

~ Knowing that I am achieving my goals

Strangely enough, some people are embarrassed by enthusiasm and try to repress it, and yet most people by far, are attracted to it.

Points to consider:

~ Do you personally agree that enthusiasm is a good thing?

~ Would you prefer to be enthusiastic all the time if you could, and

~ How would you rather spend your precious time - in the company of enthusiastic people, or with the sad sacks of society?

It breaks my heart when I recall that fewer than one third of the people that I've surveyed over the years, felt that they spent even **30%** of their waking hours, in a truly enthusiastic state, and fewer than **3%** felt that they spent as much as 60% of their waking hours in that state.

The good news is - it doesn't **have** to be that way. You know – when I think of the people queued up for their negatives – the lines go several times around the world – it just doesn't seem fair for me to want my share too, so I gift it to them and revel in all the positives that **are** out there, if only you're willing to see them.

If so few people get to spend time in an enthusiastic state though – it stands to reason that there must be some pretty serious enthusiasm

dampers out there. You need to consider your **own** list, but here are some to get you started.

The Demotivators
What are some of the things that demotivate you?

~ Feeling that you don't have any direction in your life

~ Feeling that for every step forward, you take two backwards

~ Lack of Achievement

~ Knowing that you **WANT** to make changes but being too afraid (or unsure of how) to **MAKE** them

~ Fear of loss of security

~ Fear of failure -

~ Not doing what you know you should

~ Doubt

~ Fear of the unknown

~ Expectation, and more

Fear of loss of security - for absolutely everything that we gain in this world, in some way at some time, we **will** have to pay. By far the greater majority of people want success for free - so they refuse to put their security at risk in order to take the opportunities that **are** so readily available. The problem is, this fear doesn't stop the **DESIRE**, and frustration inevitably creeps in due to lack of fulfillment.

Fear of failure - how many times have you heard the saying "what you don't know can't hurt you." So many people hide behind their fear of failure - consoling themselves by kidding themselves **and** their friends that the only reason they haven't done more with their life, is that they "didn't want to." The most damaging lie of all, is the one you tell to yourself.

Not doing what you know you should - is a disease that **everyone** suffers from at some time. The really successful people are the ones who have learned to **do** what they should, and the losers are the ones who have learned not to think about it.

Doubt - lack of confidence is a **serious** demotivator - usually fuelled by all of those other non-achievers who've convinced themselves that they were **destined** to be what they are. Heck, they don't want **YOU** to break out of the mould - you might **succeed** - and then they'd have to start convincing themselves all over again... And it's **harder** when you have the truth being flaunted under your nose!

They will come up with a million reasons as to why you shouldn't attempt to break out of the mould, with lists of people that they can point to that they "know" who tried and "failed."

I experienced that when I announced that I was moving from selling to the industrial sector, to selling a retail product. People were lining up with lists of people they had known who had tried the transition and failed. Scared the daylights out of me and for a moment I really wondered if I had made a bad decision – but then I got over it. When I really thought about the situation I wondered what could be so different – I was still selling to people after all?

So I made the change (very successfully I might add) and found both were right. As I had suspected – the selling methodology was no different but the predictability was entirely different. In the industrial sector you could forecast sales with great accuracy – month by month. In the retail sector – the month you thought you would be up would be down instead, the month you expected to be bad would be good. It was all over the place but I was glad I had made the change; for the experience I gained from it.

Fear of the unknown - admit it - change can frighten the bogies out of us. It's just easier to stay where you are. When your fear of the unknown (or of "failure") is greater than your desire to do whatever it is that you think you want to do, the result is quite simple. Nothing happens!

Isn't it interesting (once again), how many times the word "fear" comes up?

Print and read "**What vs How**"

The wonderful thing about these things is that they can **all** be changed. A great place to start in overcoming them is to focus on being the **best** that you can be, and then make it a **habit**. How do you **do** that? Well, you have to define what being the best **means** to you, and then make a check-list that you go through **each** day, to confirm that you're on your path. Be the best **you** can be - **all** the time.

So if you lack enthusiasm - what do you do about it?

You re-establish command - if you're depressed then you're not in charge.

One way of getting yourself moving is to ask yourself "If someone offered you an all expenses paid weekend on the Great Barrier Reef in Australia this weekend (subject to your getting **all** your work done) – what do you think the chances of you being up to date in time to go would be? What would you do differently, to achieve that?

So why don't you do yourself, your company and/or your family a favour, and have a weekend on the Barrier Reef **EVERY** weekend - in your mind?

It's all about attitude really (how you "see" things again). Consider the question - "Who do you work for" (**really**)? If you think about it – you may be **employed** by someone else, but you work for **you**. You work to put food on your table, to provide shelter, to "pay the bills," to be able to travel, educate yourself and so on.

Work to **your** ethics and integrity (assuming they are appropriate) and don't let a company or another person drag those ideals down. If they don't like that integrity and those ethics then you really **know** you should be looking for another company – so when are you going to start (write it in your Draft Action Plan). It is almost impossible to be happy when – eight hours a day / five days a week, you are working outside of your own acceptable standards.

To give power to your desire to **regain** command, let's take a quick peek at the damage that your depression will be doing to you. If you're depressed then:

~   Your relationships will suffer because you're not good company

~   Your health will ultimately be affected

~   Your achievement will be low in all that you do, and

~ If you're on an incentive scheme (or performance bonus) at work, then your income will likely be down too

You have to ask the question - "Are you going to let some silly psychological state of mind do all that to **YOU**? I certainly **HOPE** not!

We've looked at some of the negative effects where you're **not** enthusiastic; now let's look at some of the **positive** effects where you **are** enthusiastic.

Enthusiasm...

~ **Draws** people to you

~ Makes people **want** to listen

~ **Captures** attention

~ Aids **confidence**

~ Is **healthy**

~ Is **uplifting**

~ Is **motivating**, and

~ Is **enduring**

So **re-evaluate** those goals - maybe you've been setting them too high, maybe they aren't even yours, or maybe you haven't even got any? If you don't have goals – no problem – that's what the "Goals" chapter in this book is all about anyway.

Get **excited** about the improvement that is sure come from your new frame of mind, and remind yourself that it doesn't matter a damn what other people are doing. Measure yourself on your **own** achievements, not theirs.

The likelihood of losing your security, failing, and your lack of confidence in yourself can all be reduced to minimum levels by planning. Find out what tools you require in order to do the job in mind. Gather those tools together, learn how to use them, and as you gain in skill so your confidence will rise. The chances of failing & thereby losing your security will by now be considerably diminished, and your fears should have come down to manageable levels.

144

Don't procrastinate!!! There will **always** be a better computer about to come out; a **newer** model car, and if you wait for the perfect creation, the perfect job, the perfect husband or wife - it will never be yours.

Take the word "expectation" out of your vocabulary forever and replace it with **anticipation**. Expectation is a control issue. Expectations have a **time**, a **quality**, and a **quantity** on them, and the thing **most** likely to come out of them – is disappointment.

Where those expectations don't measure up – **disappointment** is sure to follow. My mother lived a pretty miserable life, because there was an expectation tied to almost everything she did.

Anticipation on the other hand, has no time, quality, **or** quantity attached to it – it's an unknown and therefore, is **way** more exciting than expectation.

DO WHAT YOU FEAR MOST & YOU'LL HAVE YOUR FEARS UNDER CONTROL.

Now let's get on to the good bit...

To be enthusiastic ALL the time?

Firstly, it helps if you are happy with yourself! Unfortunately some people struggle to achieve even this but thankfully, there are some universal activities that can assist here such as:

~ Creating some **direction** in your life (set some goals perhaps??)

~ **Definitely**, stop expecting yourself to be perfect. The amount of time that some people can spend beating themselves up over some perceived "failure" that isn't even important when all things are considered, would make a stone weep. I've said before that perfection is angel territory and until you have wings, you **will** get things wrong from time to time. It's perfectly "normal," and it's perfectly "okay."

~ Use this program to put **real**, living hope back in your life. Nothing, will get you more enthusiastic than seeing & believing that there is an abundance of what you want waiting out there - and that it is now within arm's reach!

~ Try **believing in yourself** and if you're really going to slack me off by saying you can't do that, then at least believe in what the people around you (that you respect), say about you. If you can't accept that you are the person that they say you are then you have no respect for them **or** their judgement. Either you accept that they are telling the truth or you need to **tell** them they are liars, and

~ Remember that no matter how bad you feel your circumstances to be, there is always something to be grateful for.

Print and read **"How Lucky We Are"**

More than anything else though...

~ To **BE** enthusiastic -

~ **ACT** enthusiastic

> To **BE** enthusiastic – **ACT** enthusiastic.
>
> *Tom Grbich*

Nothing in this world fuels enthusiasm like a smile does - especially if the smile is directed at yourself. Get out of bed in the morning, and do something really, really, **STUPID**. Stand in front of the mirror and pull faces at yourself. Sing at the top of your lungs. Turn some foot tapping music on (loud), and turn yourself loose all over the house.

If you are one of those people who wakes up grumpy then stand there in front of the mirror and **growl** at yourself!

In no time at all you will be laughing and when you can do **that**, you will find the doors to enthusiasm will be swinging wide open.

In one of my roles in a reasonably senior Management position I worked for a wonderful Multi-National company that was also terribly conservative. So on occasion I felt it was my duty to lighten things up a little.

My office was at the far end of an open plan office space and I would open my door a crack and peer out with one eyeball until someone noticed me. I'd quickly close the door and then a couple of moments later I'd do it again.

When enough people were looking, I would suddenly burst forth and do cartwheels or forward rolls to the door at the other end, and

146

disappear. (If I tried to do it now I'd probably knock myself out)! On the way back, I would run through the office at full speed, do a long dive role into my office, and close the door behind me.

People thought I was an absolute lunatic but you know; I had **heaps** of fun, **they** couldn't **help** but smile, and I'm told I was one of the most sadly missed people they had ever employed, when I moved on. Certainly I took calls for a good two years from people asking when I was going to come back and lighten them up again.

In my next role, I had a super conservative Manager who just could not be convinced to order the quantities of video recorders that I wanted.   Import license had just been freed up and we had a real opportunity to leap ahead of the opposition because we could actually **get** inventory and they couldn't.   It drove me **nuts** when I would receive information on shipments due that were 20% of what I had ordered.

Now I don't know about you but I get tremendous satisfaction out of screwing up a good crispy piece of paper. So I'd scrunch the shipping documents up in the most violent manner possible, fire them on the floor of my office and then dive under my desk with a plastic ruler for a gun. Hiding behind the rubbish bin I'd "machine gun" the bit of paper (with all the appropriate sounds) until I just had to crack up with laughter over what a fool I was being.

One day my Chinese receptionist came in as I was blasting a piece of paper from under the desk. Her eyes definitely weren't Asian for the first few moments there I can assure you! Then she regained her composure, apologised, closed the door and disappeared back to her desk.

The point is - you have to find what puts a smile on **your** face and then **DO** it - **whatever** it is (well let's not be **too** liberal here).

Eventually you'll find that you don't **need** to actually **do** those things any more - you only need to **think** about doing them and the smile will already be there. That's when you have taken real power over your life and the smile will move on to your heart.

Other things that can help you to become permanently enthusiastic include:

- **Interest** - developing an interest - whatever it may be, will draw you out of yourself and may reveal a **host** of new opportunities or new worlds to you.

- Having an **open mind** - it's important to be **open** to these new worlds - they'll lead you to discoveries, many of which will challenge your thinking, your paradigms, perhaps even your whole life to date. Discovery will lead to **learning**.

- Being **open to change** - as you learn from the new challenges you must be willing to change – yourself, your attitudes, your thinking, your behaviour, and your beliefs. Remember that if you continue to be what you've always been, the best you can hope for is that you'll continue to get what you've always got. In reality, the world is moving on and you may in fact get less and less as time moves away from you.

- **Acceptance** - accept your new beliefs - belief gives direction to enthusiasm and protects against the insecurities of doubt.

- Turn your beliefs into knowledge - if belief provides strength then knowledge provides **POWER** but **NOTE:** there is **no** knowledge without experience! So in order to turn your beliefs into knowledge – you have to **do something** with them!

Belief is merely the conclusion of a collection of thoughts or information which may (often) have no basis in reality. Knowledge comes **ONLY** with experience and once knowledge is gained, it can't be shaken or challenged. I could train you in the classroom to know more about how to defend yourself against a knife than almost anyone ever likely to attack you.

So you **believe** you can defend yourself because you understand the theory, and you've even practised the moves with the wooden knives that most people use in training to prove it. But until you're faced with a cold steel blade you don't – know - **anything**! I've known of more than one martial artist who could take a wooden knife off you before you could blink, but they died when they were attacked with the real thing. When **you**, have **done** it; **experienced** it for yourself, **then**, and **only** then are you able to say you know what it's all about. The emotional development that comes with "knowing" is immeasurable. It provides you with the strength to go on, against seemingly insurmountable odds. Do **YOU** merely believe, or do you **KNOW**?

Enthusiasm is contagious

Enthusiasm and motivation go hand in hand - if you're enthusiastic, then you will be inspired, and if you're inspired, then it would be hard not to be enthusiastic.

Enthusiasm inspires others, and makes them **want** to be with, or around you.

Now it's time to take the plunge - and I did say **PLUNGE**!! You just **CANNOT**, expect yourself to succeed in anything worthwhile in this life, by casually saying "Yeah I guess I'll give this (whatever it is) a go & if it doesn't work out - well, who cares."

Remember that the pain of the **fear** of change, typically lasts only as long as it takes to **make** the change. You'll only succeed in whatever you choose to do if you give it your best shot, and make no bones about it. You **owe** it, to yourself!

Don't agonise about it - **DO SOMETHING**!

Two of my favourite sayings are:
There are three types of people in this world

~ Those who **make** things happen

~ Those who **watch** things happen, and

~ Those who **wonder** what happened – *author unknown*

And:

All people bring joy into this world – some as they come and some as they go – *author unknown.*

In each of those cases it is worth considering where you fit.

PS – in case some of you get tied up with the "No expectations" concept – let's not be silly here. There are a (very) few things where it is totally appropriate to have expectations and I'm sure you can figure them out. As a generality though – expectation **will** lead to disappointment, so train yourself to avoid it as often as you can.

EXERCISE:

List the things that make **you** most enthusiastic in life.

Note down what **you** are going to do, to ensure you are enthusiastic just as much of the time as you want to be- in your **Draft Action Plan**.

Chapter 14

GOAL SETTING

The purpose of this chapter is to provide you with an opportunity to really put some direction in your life, by learning the importance of, and the "how to," of setting... goals.

It's important to understand before we start, that there are many things that will get in the way of your achieving the goals that you set. Perhaps the most powerful one however, is your own belief system. (Once again - remember the behaviour cycle).

By the end of this chapter you'll be able to:

~ Describe what a **real** goal is. *Of all our needs, the need to feel that we've **achieved** something - that we have personal "**value**," is one of the most sensitive. Pursuing "false" goals increases the likelihood of failure **dramatically**, and even if you **do** succeed, you might decide that goals aren't what they're cracked up to be anyway, and that would be a shame.*

~ Relate the importance of short, medium, and long-term goals. *If you're unable to relate the **importance** of short, medium and long-term goals, then it'll be harder to find a reason to set them. Equally, if you aren't convinced of the importance of measuring your progress - you probably won't. This will make it harder to stick to your longer-term goals, and once again, you're setting the grounds for perceived "failure."*

~ Begin setting **real** goals for yourself. *When you start setting "real" **goals**, you'll start seeing real **progress**. I guess that's the whole point of working with this book isn't it?*

If there was any **one** thing that could be said to have the **most** power to influence changes in our lives, that one thing would very likely be the ability to **set** goals - and more importantly, **ACHIEVE THEM.**

I have a question I'd like you to consider – "Would you class yourself as a top rated golfer?" Have you in fact ever **played** golf? Well whether you have or not, be honest with yourself now – if I told you that after only **one** minute with me – just **one** minute, I could personally guarantee that you would beat the current world champion

– would you believe me? Of course you wouldn't but the truth is - I **CAN**. All I have to do is **blindfold** the champion. You would undoubtedly win the competition now - why?

Because he no longer has anything to aim at! You **do!**

It's important that you understand that I am **NOT** being ridiculous here. This is **REALITY**. What I have just **PROVEN** to you, is that **any** unskilled person **WITH** a goal, can beat the most highly skilled person in the **world, without** one. Isn't **that** a powerful message?

The unbelievable thing for me is that no one would **contemplate** doing something as simple as playing a game of **football** without goals, yet by **far** the greater proportion of the world's population **IS** playing the game of **LIFE** without goals. No **WONDER** so many don't achieve anything in their lives. It's **FREAKY!**

I don't know about you but I've met **so** many people in my lifetime who had dreams you could paper a house with. The things they were **going** to do would make a tree stump excited. Trouble was - they never actually **DID** them. All those wonderful **ideas** never rose above being dreams.

As a result there are two things that I have nothing but scepticism bordering contempt for - **talk,** and that wonderful ethereal attribute called **"potential."** Talk and potential far too often are nothing but uncontained steam. Unless they can be translated into **action,** they might as well not exist at all. On their **own**, what you **say**, what you **think**, and whatever "**potential**" you might have, are about as much use as cars in a world without petrol. At the end of the day the **ONLY** thing that matters, the only thing that has **any** meaning, the only thing that has any **value** whatsoever in this world, is what you **DO!**

The average human being really **does** have the power to achieve whatever he/she wishes - we have **unlimited** reserves of untapped "potential." Heck even the most **conservative** estimates say we use less than one **fifth** of our brain, but the problem for most of us, comes in giving it **direction.**

In a study in America - the following findings came out:

- ~ **3%** of the population were - **independently wealthy.** *In other words, if they lost all sources of income, they could maintain their current standard of living for the rest of their lives, with no adjustments necessary.*

- ~ **10%** of the population were - **comfortable.** *If these people lost all sources of income, they could maintain a **comfortable** standard of living for the rest of their lives, with a few minor adjustments.*

- ~ **60%** of the population were – **"making a living."** *If these people lost all sources of income, they would be in real financial difficulty in a very short space of time. If the situation was at all prolonged, then they would potentially lose most if not all of their possessions.*

- ~ **27%** of the population - **needed ongoing support to survive**

Interestingly, **all** of those in the first category, had **written** goals – every one of them. Those in the second category at least had goals in mind, even if they hadn't written them down. But those in the last **two** categories had **NEVER,** ever, set goals.

APATHY STIFLES FAR MORE CAREERS, THAN INABILITY EVER WILL.

A goal is a dream – with a plan for its achievement; that is enacted to fulfilment! *Will Black.*

The rules of goal setting

- ~ Ensure that it is something that **YOU, PERSONALLY, TRULY want** out of life. *It is **useless** to pursue something just for the sake of it. Ask yourself **why** you want it, and what is going to **improve** in your life once you've achieved it.*

- ~ If it's not in **writing** then it's not a (true) goal! *Unwritten goals rarely rise above being dreams. The day that you put your goal in writing is the day that it becomes a **commitment,** that will change your life. Write **down** your goals - **list** the obstacles, **evaluate** every possible means for **overcoming** the obstacles - and **go for it.***

- ~ If it's not **specific**, then it's **not** a goal - *a vague goal such as "I* *want to be rich" is not a true goal until you've defined what "rich" means to you.*

~ It **MUST** be achievable – *saying "I want to win the lottery" is no goal at all because you have no control over its achievement. If you don't genuinely believe that you can **achieve** your goal, then you just won't apply the sweat that's required, and you'll fail before you start.*

Caution: There is a caution here however... just because a goal may not be achievable right now – doesn't mean it will always be that way. As an example, in a program that I was running some years ago, a young man expressed concern that his partially disabled son kept saying that one day he would beat his dad in a race. His worry was that it was not possible, and his son would ultimately be disillusioned as he came to realise that "fact." My comment to him was that he should encourage his son with all his heart because in his lifetime, it is entirely likely, that bio-mechanical limbs will advance to the point where his son **will** make his dream come true.

~ If it doesn't have start and finish dates then it's **not** a goal. *A time line is essential otherwise the goal may drift on forever.*

~ It must be **measurable** - otherwise *how will you **know** when you've **achieved** it?*

~ It should be a **challenge** - *if it's not something **new** and **exciting**, then again you'll find it hard to apply yourself.*

~ It must be **flexible** - *things won't always go exactly to plan so you have to be prepared to fine tune things along the way.*

~ For every long-term goal, there must be **short-term goals** along the road. *If we set a goal that's going to take five years to fulfilment, then maintaining interest is going to be a lot to expect of ourselves along the way. Short-term goals will allow you to measure your progress, and can be combined with small rewards along the way, as each minor goal is attained.*

These help too

~ Include **your family & loved ones** in your goals - they will contribute tremendously - especially if they can see something in it for them, and they can be **tigers** at keeping you on the path. In one of my Sales Management positions I was having difficulty in getting the sales people to apply themselves to attempting to over-achieve with regard to their budgets.

Even the prospect of a trip overseas to a tropical Island barely raised their eyebrows, so then I got sneaky. I wrote a letter to each of their partners explaining that if their opposite became the top performer in the next six months, they would **both** be going on a holiday to a tropical resort, and I included the glossy brochures. Man did those guys perform after that - and they complained **bitterly** that their partners were fifty times the taskmasters that I was.

~ Look at your **written goals** every day - they should be an inspiration.

~ Don't **limit your goals** - you can use your goals to plan your **whole life** if you choose. *Perhaps your goal might be... to be "different" or to **do** something different - every day.*

~ **Having** set your goals, get as **much** information as possible about what the **end achievement** entails - there can be a lot more to a goal than you realise when you start out.

I remember talking to my brother in law from my first marriage one day. He'd moved to Australia and appeared to be doing fairly well as a computer technician, but I felt that he wasn't truly settled in his life. So I asked him "Frank, what is it that you **really** want to do with your life?" He came back almost immediately with the statement that his goal was to one day own an ocean going yacht and sail around the world.

That seemed like a pretty cool goal so I asked him how he planned to support himself while doing this. He'd thought that out - he was going to earn money by chartering the yacht while in other ports. I said that was great and asked him when he was going to start sitting for his captain's license. This was met with a blank stare followed by "I beg your pardon?" So I explained that you have to be a licensed captain in order to carry paying passengers.

This made me wonder a little about how much thought he'd **really** given to this goal, so I asked if he'd given any thought to studying navigation. "No" he hadn't.

Then I asked how much such a boat would cost. He didn't know but

155

he realised "it would be a lot of money."

Really suspicious now, I asked if he had ever been out on a yacht and he laughed and said "Actually no, but I've helped a lot of my mates clean the *bottoms* of theirs." And so it ended.

Unfortunately I may have spoiled a dream for Frank, but that was all it was ever going to be anyway at the level of planning he'd done, and to my knowledge it certainly hasn't moved any closer to being a goal, since we had that conversation back in 1986.

~ Having set your goals, **PLAN THEIR ACHIEVEMENT** - a well defined plan will give you confidence and will help you to assess the achievability of your goal, within the parameters that you have set.

~ Recognise the need for **small victories** - don't set your goals too high.

~ And probably the most important thing of all - the goal/s **MUST** be **YOURS!!!** Striving for a goal that is not yours increases the potential for failure by a huge margin and you'll blame yourself, for not achieving something that was never of any real importance to you anyway.

To summarise:
Before going for **any** goal, ask yourself these questions:

~ Am I **clear** on what I want?

~ Have I set a **plan** and **a deadline** for this achievement?

~ Do I have a real **desire** for this achievement?

~ Do I have **confidence** in my ability to succeed?

~ Do I have the **determination** to succeed?

~ Is it worth the **effort** to me?

~ Am I doing this for **ME???**

Perhaps the greatest obstacle to our achievement (after belief & attitudes), is our own **conditioning**. As discussed earlier - in Burma, elephants are trained with heavy chains to restrain them, until they become accustomed to restraint. From then on, a thin piece of rope is all that's required, to prevent them from wandering.

In the plains of America there often wasn't much to tie your horse to, so the cowboys trained the horse to stay where it was when the reins were dropped to the ground. There apparently were true instances where the horse starved to death when the cowboy failed to return. Belief can be the most powerful achievement driver, and the most powerful achievement killer. It all depends, on how you use it.

Like the horse and the elephant just discussed, a lot of us similarly bind ourselves - or allow society or upbringing to do it for us.

Print and read "**How Big Your Frying Pan**"

Exercise:

In your **Personal Discoveries** page, write down some dreams that you would like to turn into goals, and then go to your **Draft Action Plan** and write down which one you are going to fulfill first.

Chapter 15

SUCCESS
It seems that if you asked, everyone in the world would tell you that they want to be a "success," but what does the word actually mean?

Objective
The information in this chapter is intended to enable you to...

~ Clarify what success means to you

~ Describe the behaviours or activities that **lead** to success, and

~ Begin defining how **you** are going to become the success that you want to be

So... what **does** success mean to you – (write it down on your **Personal Discoveries** page)?

The measures for success are incredibly diverse – for most people, success is measured by what you **have**, for others it's based on **achievement**, and for some – it's how their child describes them, when talking to a friend.

There is no "right or wrong answer" – but I'd suggest that if you measure your success by the money or assets that you've accumulated, then you're treading on **extremely** shaky ground.

There were many millionaires in Bosnia who lost everything in the war – did that mean they were no longer successful? And if your measure of success is the great job you've done in raising your family and you lose them in an accident – does that mean you are no longer successful too?

Basing your success on **anything** that can be taken away from you is a dangerous thing to do, so for me, success is not measured by what you **have** or what your title is (president, king, queen, or business entrepreneur); the **real** measure of success is **who** you are - (how you live your life).

My simple formula for becoming successful no matter what you call success is DOBD.
  D = desire

O = opportunity

B = belief, and

D = do

Success - life even, can often be compared to making a cake. There may be several ingredients that you can leave out and still have a cake at the end... less of a cake, but a cake all the same. There are **some** ingredients however that absolutely **cannot** be left out (like flour, water, and heat), and so it is with my formula for success.

Desire – desire is the fuel that will start and drive your journey **to** success. If you don't have a burning desire to have, be, or to achieve whatever it is that you have in mind, then it's unlikely that it will ever happen. Desire is the fuel that will keep you going, in the face of the many obstacles that are certain to be encountered along the way. When your desire exceeds the fear of failure; your chances of success improve enormously.

Opportunity – without opportunities, how do you make your success story real? This is where **so** many success stories remain unwritten. There **are** opportunities all **around** us, but if our eyes are closed to them then we cannot proceed, and our success will remain unfounded.

Belief – if you don't **believe** in the opportunities, or your ability to fulfill them, once again it is unlikely that you will ever see your success story come true.

Do – and finally – for any or all of the others to have any chance at all – you actually have to **DO** something. Just like the cake – you can put together the most delicious ingredients in the world but if you don't apply heat – your cake will never debut.

My mother and my father separated on their 41st anniversary having fought almost every day of their lives. In 54 years of diaries left to me when my Mum died, I found only **one** day where she wrote that she had had a really great day. **One** day in 54 years – it's the most tragic thing I have ever read. Did my parents have a **desire** for things to be different? You bet they did. On a daily basis we heard "I wish this" or "I wish that..."

What about **opportunities** you ask? Well there were many - but one I never forgot involved my father hosting the opposition political party meetings at our home, for many years. A schoolteacher, who was a regular attendee, went on to become Prime Minister of New Zealand – the Honourable Bill Rowlings. My father hated him with a passion – not because Bill was a bad person, but because every time he heard his voice, saw him on TV, or saw a picture in the paper, he was reminded that it could (and maybe should) have been him. So what went wrong?

My father didn't **believe** in himself enough. He didn't **believe** he could do it (or was **worthy** of such an achievement) and so...

He didn't **DO** anything about it.
So are **you** going to stay in your own personal hell for the next 41 years? Or are you going to go out and **do** something?
When people ask "what would I have changed in my life if I could" – it would be to have appreciated that I was never **really** alone in this world, right from the start.

What does that mean? Unfortunately, I didn't believe I **deserved** help and so I never **asked** for it.

WELL!!
What about
YOU??

Interestingly, when Microsoft was just a start-up company it caught my eye, and I wondered how you went about investing in a company like that. I even went so far as to ask my friends but they didn't know either so (you got it), I didn't **do** anything. Then in the late nineteen nineties, I saw a documentary where I found that if I **had** invested the small amount that I had planned on investing way back then, my net worth would have been close to one hundred million dollars.

Behaviours of successful people
What kinds of people do you think, who become truly successful in this world...?
~   Liars

- ~ Thieves
- ~ Slackers
- ~ Cruisers
- ~ Cowards
- ~ People who wait for others, or for "life" to create their success for them
- ~ People who blame their parents, society, or anything else they can think of for their non achievement?

What about...
- ~ Entrepreneurs
- ~ Hard workers
- ~ Visionaries
- ~ People who just won't give up
- ~ People who go beyond the call of duty just as often as it's necessary to do so
- ~ People who look at mistakes and obstacles as learning opportunities and just move on to the next success
- ~ Professionals (who act professionally)
- ~ People who take responsibility for their own lives (and problems) as early as possible in life

Which one (or combination of the above) are you? Write it on your **Personal Discoveries** page.

Professionalism is another concept that can contribute greatly to success but is equally misunderstood. Professionalism is far more about the **little** things that you do, than the **"big"** things. It encompasses...
- ~ How you dress
- ~ Your personal and work hygiene
- ~ How you treat the people around you (are you acting with genuine concern for their needs, or just walking over them)
- ~ Being on time – whether it's coming to work on time or keeping

- ~ an appointment with a customer
- ~ How you deal with problems
- ~ The language that you use, and so on

It just fascinates me that doctors regard themselves 100% as "professionals," and yet when does a doctor **ever** see you on time. And how do **you** feel about that? It's like **your** time means nothing to them. At the time of writing this manual, my charge out rate could vary from $70/hr to $400/hr depending on what I was doing, but I have sat in a doctor's office for more than an hour (**after** my appointment time), and they didn't give a damn!

A great test of how professional you are being at any given time is to ask "How would I feel if I suddenly realised that my most important customer, the head of the company, or the person I respect most in the world, was watching me right now?" If that makes you feel a little nervous, then you **know** there are some important changes that you need to consider. Go to your "**Things To Work On**" page and note down "Professionalism."

Give some thought to how professional **you** are, and what you could do to improve.

Have you ever heard of **arterio**sclerosis or artherosclerosis? It's the name given to **hardening of the arteries**.

Statistics suggest that one out of two people in this part of the world will die from cardiovascular disease - which arteriosclerosis is huge contributor to, so it's pretty serious stuff. But even worse is **psycho**sclerosis.

It's the name somebody gave to a disease that maybe three quarters of the world's population has - it causes **hardening of the attitudes**. Those people won't need to worry about dying of cardiovascular disease because they haven't learned to live anyway. They're dead from the head down, and just haven't realised it!

Success begins with **YOU** - write that down as a statement to yourself with "Me" in capital letters, and a great place to start - is with your thinking. What was the success formula again?

Desire – become **passionate** about...

~ Being the **best** that you can be – in **everything** you do, and

~ **Preparing** for your future, but **living for the day**

Believe that...

~ You **can** become whatever you want to be - within reason (sometimes time, health, and other obstacles can make certain accomplishments less likely)

~ You **deserve** to enjoy your own level of success in this lifetime

~ There **are** good people out there who will help you along the way and...

~ Stop looking at what other people can do for **you** – try thinking about what you can do for **them** for a change!

Opportunities

~ Start looking for the **many** opportunities to achieve those dreams that surround each and every one of us (if only we were willing to see them), and then...

DO SOMETHING ABOUT IT!!!

Examples of success

~ Louis L' Amour wrote over 100 Western novels and has more than 200 million copies in print but he received **350 rejections** before he made his first sale. He was the first American novelist to receive a special Congressional Medal of Honour for his contribution to writing.

~ Colonel Sanders (**at the age of 60**), made over **1,000 calls** before he found the first person willing to buy a franchise from him.

Thoughts

A couple of really important thoughts for you to finish up with...

~ The only place you'll ever find success before work is in the dictionary, and

> The only place you'll find success before work, is in the dictionary.
>
> *Originator unknown*

~ I personally have no interest whatsoever in working with people who do not want to be successful (whatever that means to them), and **neither should you**.

One of the supposed **laws** of success, is to surround yourself with successful people and while I know you **can** be successful without that – surrounding yourself with those people can certainly ease (and accelerate) your progress!

Part of what you'll discover as we go through this program is that you too are not alone, and having discovered that - what do you do with it? I have some good ideas let me assure you!

Action plan

~ Go to your **Draft Action Plan** and decide what it is that will determine success for you.   Another way of determining what success is to you, is to imagine your soul hovering above the people attending your funeral. What would you like to hear them saying about you – and why wait. Why not start living your life in a manner now, that will guarantee those words when you leave?

~ Work out what behaviours you are going to need to change (or adopt) in order to achieve that, and

~ Start **doing** something about it (now).

Note that the section on Goal Setting will be a big help here so don't hesitate to go back to it and do a review.

Chapter 16

WHAT DO I WANT MOST OUT OF LIFE
The purpose of this section is to bring your attention to the fact that so much of our inability to achieve **in** life, comes down to not knowing what we really want **from** life.

By the end of this chapter you'll be able to:
~ Describe how a lack of "direction" is perhaps the all time greatest contributor to (negative) stress (perhaps after money that is).

~ Describe the process for determining what it is that you want most out of life, and

~ Relate what it is that you are going to do, to "get it"

So what do **you** want most out of life? This is a surprisingly tough question for most people but until you figure that out, it's totally inconceivable that you could **possibly** be realising your full potential, no matter **what** you are doing!!

FAR more of the blame for any non-achievement in your past belongs here, than with your parents, your hard upbringing, or your lack of education I can assure you.

It is **EQUALLY** unlikely that you will be a "whole" person i.e. physically, emotionally, and spiritually satisfied if you haven't got an answer to this question.

The first step:
Determining just what it is that you want most out of life isn't as easy as it might sound or obviously, a lot more people would have found the answer.

The first step is to note down ideas - whatever comes into your mind that you think **might** be what you want.
~ Happiness

~ To be free

~ To have two or three really good friends that I can totally trust & rely on.

~ To be **part** of a loving caring family

~ To create my **own** loving family.

~ To be left alone - to do my own thing.

~ To be allowed to be my **own** person.

~ To be truly at one with myself, my god, the universe.

~ To be gainfully employed in a role that is challenging & allows/encourages initiative.

~ Etc. etc.

Expanding out:
Once you have a list of ideas, the next step is to analyse them. What do they actually mean and how would you know if you had achieved them?

How do you **CONFIRM** what you most want out of life? Ask yourself these questions:

~ "What is it that makes me **really** happy?" *I can't accept that there is **any** person on this planet who has not at **some** time in their life, **however fleetingly**, experienced a moment of real happiness (as they define it).*

~ "What am I doing when I feel most at **peace** with myself and the world in general?" *Once again I can't accept that there is **any** person on this planet who has not at **some** time in their life, **however fleetingly**, experienced a moment of genuine tranquility. Take yourself back to that moment and try to uncover what exactly it was, that made you **feel** that way.*

~ If this doesn't work then you must **surely** have experienced yourself observing **another** person / family / or even a **movie** that really tugged the strings of your heart. What was going on **there** that got to you? Alternatively look to your **dreams.** Surely **everyone** has their dreams, however crazy they may be and by analysis, you can often uncover what it is that you're **really** looking for in this life.

Whatever it is/was, grab it - grab hold of **anything** that may be a source, analyse it and **write** the results **down!**

Having written it down, write down what you believe you need to **do** in order to fill that gap. **Knowing** is just a waste of mental space if you aren't going to **DO** something **with** that knowledge. What you need to do will become your goal/s for life and as we discussed - unwritten goals are rarely achieved.

Everything you do IN life, should be directly linked to helping you to get whatever it is that you want most OUT of life!!

So now you know and so what? Well it's up to you - with this knowledge you can begin the process of changing your whole **direction** in life if you wish - starting with work.

> Everything you do **IN** life, should be directly linked to helping you get whatever you want most **OUT** of life.
>
> *Tom Grbich*

Draw three rectangles on a blank page – one below the other (like the diagram at the end of this chapter). In the top rectangle write down what it is that you have discovered, that you want most out of life.

In the second rectangle, note down (within the bounds of your skills and education), what **JOB** is likely to provide you with the best opportunities to **GET,** what you want most out of life?

In the third rectangle, write the name of the **COMPANY** (or companies) that is/are most likely to offer the best opportunities **within** that job, to get what you want most out of life.

Then, create a plan with respect to how you are going to **get** that job with the **right** company, and **really** get serious about changing your life.

In working with this process it is highly likely that you may discover that what you **really** want is another job (or to work for yourself). If that is the case then create a plan for this.

If you are really dissatisfied with your current job – what do you think you most need to do?

I would suggest that you need to change your thinking. Consider how your current job is going to provide you with the means to gain the **education** or the **time** (or whatever you need) in order to **find** that better job, and while you won't necessarily end up **liking** the job any more than you do now, your **attitude** towards it will likely change. It won't be such a drudge going to work in the mornings, and you will go home with more energy at the end of the day.

On the farm there were many jobs that I sure did **not** like doing, but I quickly came to realise that they were the path to what I **did** like doing - playing. If I did my jobs without being told (and did them well) I got to play, and I could also (safely) get out of sight of my parents, which meant that I was less likely to get thumped for something.

As discussed – I didn't **like** the jobs any more than before but I sure appreciated what they **did** for me, and that appreciation caused me to apply myself to them differently. The change in how you apply yourself to **your** job might even result in a promotion. Think about it!
STOP FEEDING YOUR MIND WITH GARBAGE!!

EVERY time you compare yourself unfavourably with someone else**,** **EVERY** time you tell yourself "**I** couldn't do that," you are feeding your mind with garbage. **EVERY** negative message that you give yourself of whatsoever nature, is **GARBAGE** in your mind!!

If you are **really** serious about changing your thinking but struggle with making it happen, here's an idea. Now this is pretty gross but I assure you - I am not kidding – we're talking about changing your **life** here so let's get serious!

If this is what it takes to get **you** doing what you know you **have** to do to live the life **you** want (remember it is **your** life we are talking about **not** mine, and how much did you tell me that life was worth)?

Then **do** it!

What I want you to do is get yourself one of those self sealing plastic bags, go out to the lawn and place some dog droppings or something equally disgusting in the bag, and carry it around in your pocket.

Make a **binding agreement** with yourself that from now on, **every** time you find yourself putting crap into your mind, you will take out that plastic bag and put some crap in your mouth as well. As part of

168

this agreement you do not allow yourself **any** excuses, justification or rationalisation - it's one for one! Just **watch** how quickly your attitude improves. It **works!**

I haven't had to **do** it (thank goodness), but I did have to **threaten** myself with it once and did it ever get me moving let me tell you! This is what it ultimately took, to break me out of my cycle - so I know it works.

> If you change the way you think and act, you **CAN** change **EVERYTHING,** in your life!
>
> *Tom Grbich*

If you change the way you think and act, you **CAN** change **EVERYTHING,** in your life!

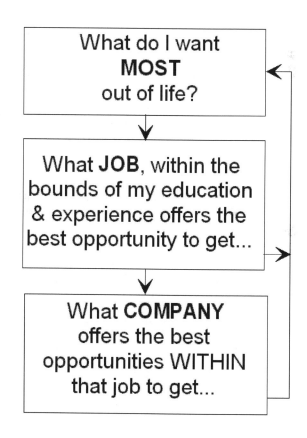

Chapter 17

BOARD OF DIRECTORS

The purpose of this section is to confirm our earlier statement that almost **no one** is **truly** "alone" in this world, and how different life can become, by taking advantage of this knowledge.

By the end of this chapter you will have:

~ Identified those people who have contributed **positively** to your lives

~ Identified those people who have contributed **negatively** to your lives

~ Identified your **current** "Board of Directors"

~ Determined who should go and who should stay, and

~ Identified whom you are going to approach to **add** to your "Board."

Essentially, this is about drawing on the people you know, to overcome the many doubts etc that will try to block your progress in this life.

Throughout our lives, we have been influenced by other people (consciously **and** subconsciously) and like a Board of Directors, some have been with us most of our lives while others may have stayed only a very short while.

Sometimes the influence will have been positive, at other times it will have been negative. Often the people will be family, but they may also be teachers, politicians, managers, partners, friends, enemies, film stars, or even fictional characters.

In fact I believe that we should have **two** Boards of Directors (appreciating that some may sit on both boards). One board would be for people with the positive **qualities** that you'd like to aspire to, and the other may be a group of people who have the business or life **skills** that you perhaps lack, and who could help with your career and/or your personal growth.

Often when I was going for job interviews, I would advise the interviewing panel that the advantage of hiring me was that they were getting more than one person. This **always** got their attention and I would then explain that in every field that I deemed myself as being less qualified or weak in, I had experts that I could call on at any time to advise me. On more than one occasion – that was what ultimately won the job for me.

Having completed this particular section as part of some training that I was providing to a major Government Department, one ambitious young manager approached me and asked if I would be "on his board." After some discussion I agreed, and he explained that he was due to have his second interview for an internal promotion that he was seeking - on Monday (this was Friday afternoon). So I told him to be at my home Saturday afternoon for the toughest interview he was ever likely to face.

Having put him through a grueling two hour interview, I then went back and told him all the areas that he had done well in, all the areas that needed improvement, and why.

Monday afternoon he phoned me to tell me that he had astounded the interview panel (made up of internal staff and external consultants) and got the job. They told him that the only reason he made it to the second interview was because he was already a staff member. In their view, he had come across as a "car salesman" in the first interview, and did not have a chance. In the second interview he was so professional that they offered him the job on the spot.

Over the next two years, he contacted me on several occasions for advice, and then did the unheard of. In a government department remember (where typically someone dies or retires and everyone moves up one), he jumped two levels of management to gain his dream job of secretary of the department in Brussels. He told me that without me on his board, it was unlikely that he would ever have had a chance.

Questions
There are three **very** important questions we must ask at this point:
1. When you look at your life to date, can you honestly place yourself in the "Chair" position currently, or have you largely

been controlled by your "board?" In other words – have you allowed others to determine your direction in life as a generality, or have you genuinely been the one to do that yourself

2. Who **are** the current members of your board (who influences you the most today), and

3. How much further could you jump ahead in your career **right now,** if you could get assistance when needed **from** that Board?

Exercise:
Drawing a picture of a boardroom table, place your name in the "chair" position and write the initials or names of the people on your current board around the table. The people who hold the most influence should be placed nearest to you.

Influence

Describe how each of those members influences you, note whether or not that influence is positive, and then consider what it is that he/she did/does to influence you.

Example: I have personally been (positively) inspired all my life by Walt Disney. He brought, and continues to bring more (healthy) joy and laughter to more people, than anyone else who has ever lived. I also admire him for the commitment he made to a dream that almost everyone around him said could never be achieved. He will remain a lifetime member of my board in spirit.

Positive qualities/valuable skills

Create a list of some of the positive qualities these board members possess (as individuals).

Examples: Caring, honest, fair, genuine, creative, committed, good sense of humour, motivated, happy, etc.

What **skills** do they possess that could help accelerate your career?

What's missing?
What skills and/or qualities do you feel you are lacking (and that are important), if you are to achieve what you now know you want out of

life?

Who

Who do you know or know **of**, that might be able to help you here (if they aren't already on your board)?

Make a list of those people and specifically, note what positive contribution you feel they could make towards the achievement of your personal and career goals. In other words (specifically) what do you **need** from them?

How

How will you go about getting these people on board if they aren't already members? What can you offer them for their contribution? Depending on who the person is (e.g. a high level business person), it may be **totally** appropriate to offer to pay them.

As long as they can see your level of commitment, most people won't accept payment - but that does not mean you shouldn't offer. In fact you should only **make** the offer if you are genuine in your willingness to reward them for their contribution.

Career

What are the next logical two or three steps in your career? If you had the right people on your board to advise you when you run into important issues that may be beyond your skills right now, could you perhaps jump directly to the second or even third step?

And... when are you going to **do** it?

In a troubleshooting role for a major car dealer in New Zealand, I went out with one of the sales people. As we were driving to his next appointment, I asked him about his plans/goals/ambitions and so on and was impressed with his (personal) financial management. He definitely had his goals and was working towards achieving them. I then asked him why he didn't apply this approach to his career.

He was a little surprised as he told me that he thought he had – so I asked him what he saw as his next career move. His response was that he felt he would be a choice for his Manager's role in about two years time. I suggested that I felt he could do that job right now and asked him how much more he felt he needed to learn in order to do so, in his view.

After some consideration he estimated about 10-15%. From what I knew of him by then - I agreed with his estimation, so I asked him how far he would need to extend himself to jump to the next level above that.

*This time he felt a 40-50% learning shift would be likely and I again agreed with his estimation. So I asked him why he would consider waiting two more years for a role that he could do now, and spend another two to four years doing **that** job before going on to the job of his choice? I believed he could make the jump right now, and save perhaps 5 years.*

That made him nervous and he said "Well I don't feel I could handle it right now." I replied – "You are right, but who do you know that you could call on for assistance, with the 40-50% of the role that you are unsure of at this point?"

He immediately started coming up with names and after a slight pause, turned and asked if I would be on his board too. I agreed, and he soon took the jump – moving years ahead in his career.

Whose board

With or without knowing it, there will be people whose board of directors **you** sit on - children for sure. Make a list of whom those people might be.

What contribution

What **positive** contribution do you make to the achievement of **their** goals, and/or the quality of their life?

Is it at all possible that your contribution is **not** so positive? If so – what will you do to change that?

What more **could** you be doing in this role? What **will** you do from here on?

Learn

What have you learned from this exercise? Write it down.

Review

Effective CEO's review the performance and value of those on their board with established regularity. Those who are contributing positively are retained, and the others are replaced.

When was the last time you reviewed **your** board? How will you proceed from here?

In the event that you choose to introduce this concept into your life; how many boards will you have, and how regularly will you review the members of those boards? Remember that people don't even have to know that they are **on** your board but if they **do** know, they will often contribute a lot more.

Write it down (in your **Draft Action Plan**)

Chapter 18

PERSONALITY TYPES
Print and fill out "**Identify Your Style**"

Appreciating that while from the point of view of "needs," we are all very similar - we are also different, when it comes to personalities.

By the end of this chapter you'll able to:
~ Describe the four main personality types

~ Relate at least three methods that you can use to determine each of the four types when you come in contact with them

~ Describe the adjustments you will need to make in order to deal with each of the personality types, and

~ Describe the primary turn ons vs the primary turn-offs, of each of the personalities

We're different? Don't be confused – when we discussed "Needs" it was made apparent that we are "**not** so different" and now we are saying we **are**?

Actually, your information remains entirely accurate – human needs are similar across the board, but as we all know – personalities are not.

Personality styles are used all over the world, but they typically end up being of little more use than a good horoscope – why is that?

The big problem with all of these tools is that before you can determine the changes that you might need to consider making in order to know how to deal with someone, you first have to put them through the process. That is often not possible.

The other problem is that the style descriptors of many of the profiling tools are extremely difficult to remember and relate to.

Quite simply – it just becomes "too hard."

In considering these issues, I asked myself "What is it that we really

176

need to know about people, in order to build quicker, easier, more, lasting relationships, and have better communication with them?"

If you think about it, the old statement "Do unto others as you would have them do unto you" is not very good advice. If will only serve you if the other person is **like** you! If I was a sexual pervert and started "doing unto you that which I would love you to do unto me" – I probably wouldn't make too many friends out there.

My version says "do unto others as they would **have** you do unto them" and if you do this – I guarantee you will be far more successful. But how do you do unto others as they would have you do unto them - if you don't know who they are? Quite simply, we need to know...

M.O.R.E.

We need to know "more" about the person:
~   Do they like to be touched - do they prefer "hands off"

~   Do they appreciate a fast pace or a slow one

~   Do they like lots of detailed information to work with, or

~   Are they conceptual

~   Do they like to make quick decisions or do they prefer time to think

~   Do they prefer a formal approach or an informal one, and so on

Power
Before proceeding, I would like to tell you how powerful this information can be.

When I first moved to Canada I worked with a wonderful guy who was a qualified trainer in the DISC system (interestingly), and one day we were out together when he started talking about problems he was having with his (14 year old) son.

As the conversation went on, I asked him to describe his son to me, and the problem was immediately apparent. I told him his problem was that he was a high (about 18) Monkey, and his son was a medium high Eagle (about a "14") on my scale of 20. Eagles don't have a lot of respect for Monkeys so if he wanted to improve communication with his son – he needed to bring a little "Eagle" into his behaviour.

My friend did as suggested and was so impressed by the result that he put his whole family through the DISC system, and everything changed for the better in the process.

So the basic personality types that you will use from here on are the:
~ Monkey

~ Owl

~ Retriever, and

~ Eagle

And the information that you are going to receive is totally compatible with the more expensive computer derived profiles such as DISC, Myers & Briggs, and so on.

The **Monkey** personality is referred to in other programs as *Influencing / Extrovert / Persuader / Activist etc*

The **Owl** is referred to as *Compliance / Conforming / Conservative / Theorist*

The **Retriever** is referred to as *Steadiness / Tolerant / Introvert / Reflector,* and

The **Eagle** is referred to as *Dominance / Controlling / Driver / Pragmatic*

The Monkey is the "extrovert, activist, flamboyant" personality – hot buttons – recognition, inclusion in all that is going on, variety, freedom.

The Owl is the "theorist, thinking, calculating" personality – hot buttons - detail and information.

The Retriever is the "tolerant, conforming, passive" personality – hot buttons - warm fuzzies, nurturing, caring.

The Eagle is the "dominant, autocratic, pragmatic, controlling" personality – hot buttons - power, results, and control.

Note: It is absolutely vital that we understand that this is not a "good versus bad" personality contest. Personalities just "**are**" and each has its area of excellence. It is also important to appreciate that we'll be dealing with personalities in the "**pure**" sense, which is not how things work in reality. We all have **some** of the characteristics of the other styles and it's the levels, and the combination of styles, that will ultimately define the person that others see.

As a generality, people will have a dominant style and a supporting style that sometimes are very close, while the other two styles tend to measurably fall away. The supporting style or styles have a significant impact on the primary style, strengthening or softening – dependent on what the styles are. Given the chance however (and particularly under stress), the dominant style will usually come to the fore.

Levels
In general - the higher the level of the primary style, the less able the person is to adapt, while a lower level generally indicates more flexibility. People whose styles are lower (each characteristic below 10 for example), tend to be chameleons – it's really hard to tell **what** they are, and often they will be confused themselves.

It is important to note that any one of the styles can change dramatically in its level, to suit circumstances at the time. The warm, nurturing, loving Retriever for example, can become a raging Eagle in the event that someone threatens someone they love. Most people make changes to their profile to cope with what they perceive as being the different aspects of themselves required by work.

The important thing to note is that it has been proven that if you are making changes of greater than 20% in any part of your profile for periods of longer than three months at a time - you **WILL** get sick! You'll almost certainly be aware of the stress that you are under, and that stress will ultimately have you catching colds, the flu, and worse!

Another thing...
Another thing to consider is that often people going through this section will be unsettled – they want to be more "Monkey," or more

"Eagle" etc... It is **so** important that you don't let your ego do this to you. As discussed – there are no "good" or "bad" styles – you are what you are. **Every** style has its strengths and weaknesses – concentrate on the strengths of **your** primary style, and look at what you can do to overcome the weaknesses.

Note that the personality descriptions are based on a person being "high" (18+) in that modality. The lower the level, the less extreme their behaviour will be.

Monkey (Extrovert, Activist, Influencing)

General comment

We'll look at the some of the more recognisable characteristics of the

Monkey in a moment but as a generality, the "Monkey" loves people - and being the centre of attention. Their genuine interest in people makes others regard them as being amazingly friendly, because shyness is not a word that you'll find in their vocabulary. Monkeys **love** being around other people, and they're often "technically challenged" in the extreme.

"Monkeys" have an almost intuitive ability to "read" people well, they're genuinely empathetic, and their explanations are full of stories. They are excellent at putting others at ease; they enjoy teamwork, and involvement with people.

They **love** to talk and generally, they prefer to talk rather than to write things down.

Sometimes it appears that the "Monkey" has little regard for discipline – they just want to relax and play. As long as you're not hurting anyone – rules? shmules – let other people worry about them.

Human conflict causes real pain to the "Monkey" - they want everyone to just be "one big happy family." In certain circles this can be taken advantage of because they're more willing than most, to enter into compromises that may not be particularly beneficial to them.

As leaders, "Monkeys" may try too hard to please everyone - trying to "keep the peace" and in doing so, they sometimes avoid taking the "hard line" or making the unpopular decision that may be more appropriate for the circumstances. "Monkeys" are often taken advantage of by stronger, more dominant personalities like "Eagles," because of their willingness to give in to the wishes of others, in order to please them. Fortunately, "Monkeys" don't seem to care who is in charge.

"Monkeys" demonstrate their "harmonising" personality on a daily basis. They're the ones who always say, "Have a nice day" (and **mean** it), and it would surely have been a "Monkey" who invented the "smiley face" on company memos. "Monkeys" wilt in solitary jobs; they **must** be out working with people.

"Monkeys" are often nature lovers, adore their pets, have large circles of friends, and tend to be excellent "human" problem-solvers.
Although the "Monkey" shares their qualities freely with others, they're not always as kind to themselves. When things go wrong, "Monkeys" tend to blame themselves first, sometimes to the point of becoming severely depressed. This trait is the one that is most damaging to the "Monkey" and one that they have to remain on guard about.

Recognisable characteristics
Some of the more recognisable characteristics of the Monkey are:

~ Their persuasiveness

~ Their warmth - they will want to know your name and use it a lot in conversation

~ Even under duress they always keep the feelings of the other person in mind

~ They appear cheerfully optimistic - always able to see a positive side to a situation

~ They'll be very clear in their explanations of their "situation" and will try to lay guilt trips rather than shout at you

~ Their empathy

~ Their enthusiasm

~ They can almost always find something to talk about

~ They are excellent mixers

Their verbal communication will be:
Full of stories & anecdotes, informal and descriptive. It will involve their personal feelings and will often go off on tangents. It will involve lots of pitch variation, be fast paced, high volume and have a definite flair for the "dramatic." The following words/statements will appear often in their conversation.

~ Lovely / nice / I feel / my gut feel / complimentary / comfortable / co-operate / team

~ Do you have children...?

~ How is the family...?

~ We're just a big happy family around here...

~ Can we chat about this...?

~ Let's just sit down and talk this through...

~ People are our most important product...

~ How can we get around this Shelley...?

~ Craig what can we do to short circuit this...?

~ I'm sure you will sort this out - Sandra wasn't it...

~ You know what we need...

~ I'm sure you wouldn't want...

~ I have full confidence in you...

~ It will spoil our whole trip if we can't get around this...

~ It will be so disappointing if we...

~ We don't have a lot of time so what can I do to help you with this...? and,

~ I **know** we can beat this if we work together...

Primary turn on
The primary turn on for the "Monkey" is positive recognition/being with other people.

Fear
The greatest fear of the "Monkey" personality is to be left out of the goings on.

Appearance
The male "Monkey" personality tends to dress "casual" with an emphasis on comfort. They're not into the three-piece suit scenario, preferring sports jackets or sweaters with leather elbow patches, open necked shirts and no ties. The "Monkey" male likes "earth" colours - browns, greens, and blues with the occasional tan or burgundy thrown in. They often look younger than their age, with a noticeable absence of "worry" lines.

The "Monkey" female also prefers casual attire - particularly loose fitting clothes, which feel nice on the skin. They like sweaters, Angora, light wool products with full flowing skirts, and blouses with bows and "fluffs" - anything that offers the "natural" look.

They do go for painted fingernails and strong perfumes, and hair tends to be either short and curly, or very long.

Body language
Typical body language indicators of the "Monkey" include:
~ They smile a lot

~ They're very animated in expressions and gestures

~ They will concentrate on you intensely when in communication

~ They will use eye contact to the point of making you uncomfortable

~ They nod a lot in confirmation of what you and/or they are saying

~ They tend to be the touchers and huggers of the personality styles

~ They often use the two handed handshake or will place their left hand on your shoulder as they shake your hand

~ They rarely move slowly - their usual pace is a bouncy stride that gives the appearance that they're going somewhere exciting, even when they aren't

Office
The "Monkey" office looks like a home. It will be decorated with lots of live plants, and the colours will be soft or "earth" tones. Often the workspace will be somewhat disorganised, with papers strewn about haphazardly. Photos of people goofing off together - often from the Christmas work party will be seen, and usually there will be more than one photo of the family. Above all it will be a "comfortable" space.

Building rapport, dealing with, the "Monkey"
If you want to build rapport with the "Monkey" personality, **use an emotional approach** and:
~ **Invite conversation** – get them chatting – "Where are you going, how long will you be away, where did you hear about this?"...

~ Give them your **full attention** and show "real" interest in them

~ Don't be afraid to ask what others might class as "personal" questions - they **love** to talk about themselves and their "situation"

~ **Be enthusiastic**

~ Give them an opportunity to get "involved

~ Use superlatives like "that sounds fantastic, great, awesome, wonderful..."

~ Appear cheerfully confident - "This shouldn't take too long; that shouldn't be a problem... I'll have this sorted out by..."

~ Use illustrations to make your point

~ Appear as though you are having fun

~ Offer tea or coffee, and

~ Let them know how important it is and that others think it is too

More than anyone else, the "Monkey" loves to have a follow-up call.

Lead to a decision

Lead ins to decision making for the "Monkey" might follow the lines of...

~ We could really use you on the team - how would you feel about that?

~ When would you see yourself coming on board?

~ It would be great if you could get involved because then you would be part of the "family"

~ If you like team spirit then this is the way to go

~ It would be a real shame if you were unable to proceed, or

~ What would you need from us to make you want to get involved in this?

Under stress

~ Typically, the "Monkey" will either attempt to pretend the situation doesn't exist, or get (very) emotional & panic (loudly), while moving around a lot so as to gain the biggest possible audience.

Indicators

When the "Monkey" is under stress they may appear:
- More manipulative and less "people" focused
- Even noisier
- More impulsive
- More dependent on support from others
- Superficial, and
- Unrealistic

Helping them

If you hope to quickly bring them back to productivity they will need:
- Action and interaction
- A quick pace for stimulation
- Reassurance of relationships, and
- Some positive recognition

Do not

You will lose them if you:
- Get too carried away with the "facts"
- Get bogged down in "detail" or "procedure"
- Sound unenthusiastic, or
- Make it sound like it is going to be "complicated," or a "big deal"

Owl (Conforming, Conservative, Theorist)

General comment

"Owl" personalities are cautious in their actions and decisions because being "right" is very important to them. They enjoy organisation and structure in every aspect of their lives (as long as it makes sense), and they pay meticulous attention to detail. They need life to be predictable; everything in the right place at the right time.

They like lots of time to plan, and prepare for the unexpected. The "Owl" tolerates people but generally feels the world would be a better place without them (other people) so understandably, they dislike "involvement."

The most dominant characteristic of "Owls" is their determination to get the job done. If you need a task accomplished, turn to an "Owl" every time. No matter **what** is involved or how long it takes, once they're committed to it, they'll persevere to the bitter end!

"Owls" are strong administrators because of their almost compulsive attention to detail. The "Owl" loves to collect information, enter it into a database, or file it under the appropriate heading so that it's properly organised.

Of course, with every set of strengths, there are a few weaknesses also. The "Owl" tends to be better at **following** a plan than designing one and they make better administrators than managers. The problem comes from their need to be "right" and where risk is involved, they freak at the thought of making a "wrong" decision.

"Owls" do **not** function well in situations that aren't defined, or that are in a constant state of flux. Where instructions and requirements are clear though, the "Owl" excels above all the other styles.

The "Owl" is usually an extremely knowledgeable person – they read lots of factual material and they have a strong preference for watching documentaries.

Their approach is **very** analytical (to the point of analysing things to death), they ask lots of questions of a very detailed, technical nature, and they prefer an objective, task orientated work environment.

Emotion is something the "Owl" rarely shows personally, and something they prefer to avoid in other people. Their views and values tend towards the 'very traditional' and they're compulsively logical and practical.

Perfection is the only thing the "Owl" can relate to and this element along with their distaste for emotional situations, can lead them to be seen as cold, aloof, and as "loners."

They absolutely **hate** having their work criticised and often take that **very** personally, and they prefer information and/or instructions in writing.

People with the "Owl" personality type can be identified by their tendency to be highly sensitive to anything that could be deemed to be criticism of them, and their penchant for taking things personally.

When things aren't going their way or they've taken offence to something they tend to get "huffy" rather than angry. If you **really** piss them off though, they'll storm away and gather **every** item of supportive information they can get their hands on and "**nail you**" on their return.

Character indicators
Quick character indicators for the Owl are:
~   Love of detail

~   They like procedure

~   They tend to be formal, and prefer others to be that way too

~   They like things in writing

~   Owls are very strong on accuracy

~   They're very "precise" in everything they do

~   They like preordained standards and systems

~   Owls like to know what to do, when to do it, and how to do it

188

~ They're strong on rules and structure, and

~ They will try to keep a "safe distance" between themselves and other people

Personal traits

Some of the more recognisable personal traits of the "Owl" include:

~ Being extremely careful in everything they do

~ They are highly dependable and very loyal

~ They are perfectionists

~ They tend to be very conservative

~ They're natural "worriers"

~ They're (very) sensitive to criticism

~ They prefer tradition and are very much "creatures of habit"

~ They want to know all the details and facts

~ They often come across as "formal and reserved"

~ They're very resistant to change and risk taking

~ They respect leadership and are **very** loyal to "good" leaders

~ They just **hate** making mistakes

~ They may resist being "tested"

~ They go "by the book"

~ More than most, they tend to believe what's in writing, and

~ They're slow to make friends

Their verbal communication will be:

Relatively quiet, slower paced with little pitch variation, and will be delivered in a steady almost monotone way, using (typically) unspecified" words/statements like:

~ Analysis, logistics, organise, allocate, assign, monitor, deadline, project, plan, efficiency, right, accurate

~ The policy clearly states...

~ We've always done it this way...

~ That's not my problem/job

- If you want a job done properly - do it yourself

- Now what **exactly** do we need to do...?

- Send me all the details on this...

- What is the procedure for...?

- Surely you can...

- Would you be able to put this in writing...?

- I'm sure we didn't have to do this last time... or

- I'm sure our friends didn't have this problem when **they** did this...

Primary turn on
The primary turn ons for the "Owl" are lots of intellectual information, and to be left alone.

Fear
The greatest fear of the "Owl" personality is to be proven "wrong," or to have to socialise with a group of "emotional" people (Monkeys for example).

Appearance:
The "Owl" personality is likely to be even more conservative in their dress than the "Retriever." Men prefer dark suits with a white handkerchief protruding from the pocket, and white shirts. Hair is usually short and they are usually well shaven. Alternatively, they'll have a heavy beard and long hair. They tend to carry a comb in a side pocket with a lint brush in the briefcase or the desk drawer, and shoes are shined on the same evening every week.

They buy at the same men's shop and insist on being served by the same sales person each time.

Women shop at medium priced department stores and go for "full outfits" for a complete season at one time. Colours are usually black, brown, grey, or navy and there is very little variety to be found in their wardrobe. Shoes are focused on comfort rather than style; hair is either short or in a very "controlled" hairstyle.

Body language

Typical body language indicators of the "Owl" include:

~ Very few gestures or mannerisms

~ They tend to perspire a lot in situations requiring social contact

~ Expressionless face - **especially** in emotional situations

~ Their body appears very stiff and when sitting, they almost never slouch (at least not in the presence of others)

~ Jerky movements when they're uncomfortable

~ They rarely run - their movement is usually slow and purposeful and if they're required to hurry, it is a very "controlled" pace (like running in slow motion)

Office

"Owls" like a strong (preferably real wood) desk, which will be meticulously tidy and organised. Policy or technical manuals are the preference for bookshelves. A single-family photo may be in evidence, and the walls will be lined with awards, certificates and plaques. Diplomas will also hold pride of place in the "Owl" office but the focal point will be the personal computer. In general, the "Owl" office can best be described as sterile.

Building rapport, dealing with, the "Owl"

If you want to build rapport with, with the "Owl" personality:

~ Be logical

~ Be serious and formal

~ A firm, formal handshake is all that is required - they want to be your customer, not your friend at this point

~ Don't smile too much or be too exuberant - they'll wonder what you're "on"

~ Use direct eye contact and don't talk too much. Owls are perfectly comfortable with long silent periods and that usually indicates that they're thinking

~ Pay strong attention to detail - they like lots of features/benefits information and as a "special" you could even show them the manual. Be warned that they might want to read it though

~ **Never** try to bluff an "Owl." They're very intellectual people and may already know the answer to the question they're asking. If they catch you out they won't tell you - they just won't buy from you – **ever**

~ Be very careful about using any "personal" questions. "Owls" tend to be **very** private and this will turn them off dramatically

~ Emphasise "fairness"

~ Show them "guarantees"

~ Provide lots of facts and detail

~ Give them lots of material to read if they want to "reserve their decision," and

~ **Put it in writing**

Lead to a decision
Lead ins to decision-making for the "Owl" might follow the lines of...

~ You can see how fairly priced this is...

~ Look at the thoroughness and detail that has gone into...

~ You'd be amazed at the research that has gone into this...

~ Can you see how this would be the right decision for...

~ The accuracy and precision of this...

~ I'm sure this would improve your ability considerably in relation to meeting time constraints...

~ The facts are right there...

Under stress
Under stress, typically, the "Owl" personality will get huffy and withdraw - perhaps becoming downright reclusive – burying themselves in work or research.

Indicators
When the "Owl" is under stress they may appear:

~ Even more reliant on data collection

~ Defensive in the extreme

~ More resistant to change

- ~ Slower to act

- ~ Slower to begin work

- ~ Unable to meet deadlines

- ~ Unimaginative

- ~ Resentful, and

- ~ They will rigidly follow "the rules"

Helping them

If you hope to quickly bring them back to productivity they will need:
- ~ Assurances that they're right

- ~ Understanding of principles and details

- ~ A slow pace for processing, and

- ~ Assurance of information accuracy

Do not

You will lose them if you:
- ~ Get too "big picture"

- ~ Speak "conceptually

- ~ Gloss over the "fine print"

- ~ Indicate that you are more concerned with "the way it is" rather than what is fair, or

- ~ Give the impression that you are "exaggerating" in any way

Retriever (Tolerant, Introvert, Reflector)

General comment

The "Retriever" personality is usually **really** easy to get along with. They have a strong need to be liked and will go to great lengths to  avoid anything that may cause others to dislike them. They do little to promote themselves, feeling that the attention they get might cause others to resent them, and while they often have very good ideas they may have to be "pumped" to get those ideas out. Paradoxically, they're often **extremely** resentful about having been "overlooked." They feel that Management should be able to "see" how good they are at their job and what great workers they are, and offer promotion to them on that basis.

The Retriever is usually exceptionally reliable and will do almost **anything** for other people. They **will** accept leadership positions because of the recognition, but they're often not entirely comfortable in the role - especially if it means having to deliver "bad news" to others.

The "Retriever" tends to be a fairly serious, "thinking" personality who enjoys a good joke but not if it's directed at them. They have **excellent** analytical skills and enjoy learning - as much to impress others as to fulfill their own genuine interests.

One of their strengths is in the very logical, rational manner in which they approach problems. Their ability to analyse, judge and discriminate is usually well developed but at the end of the day, they may struggle to actually make a **decision**, where it contradicts with what they "feel."

They display a strong concern for the betterment of both their immediate community and the world around them. When matters are important to them (or to please someone), they often work as long as it takes to get the job done, giving generously of their time, money and energy when there's any chance of assisting others.

The "Retriever" spends a lot of time in a "dissatisfied" state of mind.

194

They **know** things can/should be better but they lack the drive or perhaps the confidence, to go out and **make** it happen. They may show **incredible** patience with others while often being exceptionally **im**patient with themselves. They beat up on themselves something terrible, and while they do tend to have a fairly long fuse, when the fuse burns out - look out.

Some volcanoes simmer and boil - belching smoke from time to time and even spewing out lava on occasions. Others sit in silence for thousands of years then blow themselves and everything near them to pieces. If volcanoes had personalities, the latter would be the "Retriever"- sitting there quietly taking in everything that life throws at them - in a state of "dormancy," and then without any external indications except to the most sensitive people (or instruments) - bang. And when they blow, it's an explosion to remember. **Years** of frustration come boiling out and you may cop lots of "stuff" that you never had anything to do with, or that you certainly don't remember.

Under normal circumstances they give the outward appearance that nothing really bothers them and they just "roll with the punches" as life goes on, but "Retrievers" **never** forget an injustice. In a sense they're dishonest because they will rarely ever let you know how they **really** feel.

If you ask how they are, the traditional answer will be "Not too bad" or "Oh pretty good" when in fact they may be feeling anything but. In extreme cases they'll just burst into tears – leaving you wondering, "What on earth did I just say?"

Retrievers are slow to take action and make decisions because they're afraid of how they'll "look" if they do the wrong thing, and they're always trying to anticipate how their decision might impact on others. They like close personal relationships and while they're **very** supportive, interestingly, they're often **not** good listeners. Trying too hard to "relate" to the other person, they often frustrate people by comparing problems **they've** had, and the conversation ends up on them.

Retrievers don't often do well at doing things for themselves - they work best where they have someone to please.

Retrlevers work slowly and cohesively with others, and "security and belonging" are their primary needs. They have a definite preference for being with others, as opposed to being alone.

Character indicators
Quick character indicators for the Retriever are:
~ Even when stressed they appear very controlled and calm

~ They tend to be very nurturing/caring by nature

~ They tend to be "quiet" natured until they get to know you and then they'll often talk the leg off a chair

~ They develop strong attachments with people

~ They're inclined to be perfectionists

~ They tend to be very sentimental

~ They have a **strong** dislike of change

~ They're usually **very** patient

~ They're moderate in taste and manner

~ They tend to hold things "inside"

~ They're easily hurt and will try to make you feel "sorry" for them, and

~ They think (often very carefully) before they speak.

Personal traits
Some of the more instantly recognisable personal traits of the "Retriever" include:
~ They're very consistent

~ They're **extremely** tough on themselves when they think they have made a mistake, or especially if they think they have let someone down

~ They like to be on time or preferably early

~ They love to "help out"

~ They have a "nervousness" about them (they fidget)

~ They listen intently and will rarely commit themselves to a statement without support

~ If/when they do make a statement it will be along the lines

196

~ of "I was wondering how it would be if we did it ... way - what do you think?"

~ They're real packrats - can't throw anything away because "it might be useful one day"

~ They avoid anything that looks like conflict unless they can come out looking good to all parties

~ Retrievers "ask" or "make suggestions" rather than "tell."

~ They (generally) listen more than they talk

~ They tend to "reserve decisions" till they're more assured of support, and

~ They prefer large groups because it's easier to be invisible

Their verbal communication will be:
Slower, quieter, question filled, with typically kinaesthetic words or statements like:

~ I'm not sure

~ I feel bad about this

~ Oh no...

~ What do you think

~ Oh that's terrible...

~ What am I going to do...?

~ This is really a problem for me...

~ I thought all I would have to do was...

~ I... suppose so

~ Should I take notes?

~ Can I get back to you?

~ I'm not sure...

~ Could you go over that again...?

~ There's a lot to think about

~ What are the alternatives

Primary turn on

The primary turn on for the Retriever is love. To make them happy show them you care, make them feel wanted and make them feel "safe."

Greatest fears
Perhaps the greatest fears of the "Retriever" personality are conflict, and to be disliked.

Appearance
The "Retriever" personality tends to dress very conservatively with a preference for browns and other "warm" colours. They're self-conscious about wearing "brand names" or expensive clothes - and often remain miles behind the current fashions. They generally are very meticulous with their appearance however - often to the point of not a single hair being out of place. They can take simply **ages** to get ready and the result rarely **ever** matches the time spent.

Body language
Typical body language indicators of the "Retriever" include:
~ A raft of "nervous" habits such as "clearing the throat, scratching, stroking their face or hair, eye or facial twitches, or clicking ball point pens"

~ They tend to be uncoordinated and clumsy when nervous - dropping and bumping into things

~ They give fleeting eye contact

~ They tend to look down a lot

~ You can have long silent periods with a Retriever

~ Nervous giggles

~ Gestures tend to be short, and movements small, and

~ Their favourite position when standing waiting, is with one hand holding the other at crotch level in front

Office
No matter how busy they are, the Retriever will always have a meticulously tidy office and will always know exactly where everything is. Mess = stress. They're very proud of their office and will spend a lot of time there even when there isn't a lot to do. When seeing people in the office they will usually keep the desk as a barrier not to

198

exert power as the "Eagle" does but because it makes them feel "safe."

Building rapport, dealing with, the "Retriever"
If you want to build rapport with the "Retriever" personality, use an emotive approach and:

~ Give indications of your trustworthiness, your honesty

~ Show real interest in them

~ Talk about "safety" & "security" in a slow and relaxed manner

~ Discuss how you like things to "go smoothly"

~ Give them options and alternatives

~ Indicate how their personal circumstances will be positively impacted

~ Imply that you like to have things happen on time

~ Be warm & caring

~ Use quiet persuasion

~ Show references from "important people"

~ Gently probe to learn as much as possible about their needs

~ Show concern (for them) when you detect signs of confusion

~ Be as clear as possible in your explanations

~ Be patient

~ Use a relaxed and easy going style

~ Use lots of positive statements, and

~ Let them know how thrilled you'll be if they're able to do what you want

Lead to a decision
Lead ins to decision-making for the Retriever would follow the lines of...

~ From our discussion I'm sure you can see how this will keep things going smoothly.

~ When do you imagine yourself going ahead with it?

~ Where do you see this benefiting your organization?

~ Won't people be surprised when...?

~ This will tidy things up for you...

~ When do you think this would best fit in with your plans?

Under stress
Under stress, typically, the "Retriever" personality will get emotional (perhaps to the point of tears), and submit.

Indicators
When the "Retriever" is under stress they may appear:
~ Wishy washy

~ Submissive

~ Passive

~ Dependent

~ Hesitant

~ Defensive, and

~ Even more indecisive

Helping them
If you hope to bring them back to productivity they will need:
~ Reassurance that they're liked

~ Personal assurance

~ Slow pace for comfort and security

~ Relationships that they can be confident in

Do not
You'll lose them if you:
~ Rush them

~ Make sudden changes, or

~ Appear to be "pressuring" them

Eagle (Dominant, Controlling)

General comment

As suggested by the title, these people like to be in control. "Eagles" are achievement and goal oriented; they're ambitious, and they aim for high places.

Eagles admire those who achieve, and struggle to understand those who aren't similarly driven to do so. *As an example, a high "Eagle" that I once worked for was at a social function with his wife. Somehow the conversation turned to relationships and the "Eagle" publicly stated that if it came to a choice between money and marriage – money would be the natural choice.* Then, noticing tears in his wife's eyes he turned and said "What the hell's wrong with you?"

They're individualistic and independent.

Their strong need to prove to themselves and the world that they're good at what they do - often leads them to be adventurous, entrepreneurial, and **highly** competitive. *The same person mentioned above was a classic. Any new staff member soon learned that if they wanted a life, then don't beat the boss at squash. If you did, you could expect to be back there every night until he finally beat you.*

Challenge brings out the best in them. Independent and self-assertive, they tend to dominate both situations and people. They **love** authority and while being naturally opportunistic, they **dislike** uncertainty, preferring to resolve problems or settle situations quickly – one way or another.

They seek recognition and tend to be serious in nature; they're generally good long-range planners, fast decision-makers, and very hard workers. They never seem to tire - preferring a high workload, with scope for lots of activity.

People high in the "Eagle" personality are the doers of this world. They **need** action - they're self-starters, **loaded** with self-confidence, and strong on initiative. They're generally good problem solvers and "ideas" people. Around others they're usually factual, to the point, direct *(some would say blunt,)* and outspoken.

Eagles are good at getting results, getting things moving, accepting challenges, making decisions, questioning the status quo, taking authority, and solving problems.

High doses of this trait though, often lead to opinionated, arrogant, unfeeling, and closed-minded people - sometimes to the point of being downright pig-headed. They may be argumentative, and very often, human relations skills are something they believe belong in Disneyland.

They believe they're right - when very often they're wrong - making decisions too impulsively, and **acting** in the same manner. Consequences may include costly blunders, while making life miserable for their subordinates. They mistake "action" alone as being important.

Often they're **hopeless** delegators, failing to provide proper instructions, support, follow up, and/or coaching, and expecting results, but rarely reflecting on whatever it is that they've delegated.

Communicating their expectations to employees is **not** one of their skills. When asked a question they'll often answer with, "You're a smart guy/girl – you'll figure it out," and then they react with abject astonishment, when you come back with something different than what they were expecting.

Unfortunately, with little empathy for people, they can be hopeless people managers, with little if any ability to motivate others, other than by fear.

They are notoriously bad listeners, often offering only token attention to others, and communication tends to be a one-way street.

Aggression comes naturally and in worst cases, they aren't just controlling, but downright domineering, without ever realising it. Their lack of empathy tends to make them blissfully unaware of their impact on others.

Eagles can be bitingly critical and sometimes that criticism is delivered thoughtlessly, in public.

They often don't understand the basic law of physics which also applies in human relations - "To every action, there is an equal and opposite **re**action" resulting in difficulties in retaining staff.

Their intolerance of other people's views, methods, and level of performance means that they rarely stop to question **why** performance is low, or how **they** might have contributed to it - it's more a case of "She's not working out - she'll have to go."

Consequently they often fail to support the very people who need their coaching and leadership most of all.

Ironically, they're often ultra sensitive to any criticism of themselves, their judgments, or their performance. This may cause them to be brutal with employees who (in their minds) speak up too much. If you don't agree with them, then you're against them.

Eagles often form prejudices that are lasting, leaving the employee against whom they have the bias with no choice but to leave the company. Eagles are often the primary cause of employee turnover because their employees fire **them,** by leaving to work for someone else!

Although they share the left-brain orientation of the "Owl", "Eagles" are less interested in the work than they are in their career. The "Eagle" is ambitious and his/her personal focus is on reaching the top.

Perhaps the single most valuable trait of the "Eagle," is their ability to focus on the goal of the moment and they always know what the goal is, because unlike the "Owl", the "Eagle" is a very decisive person. "Eagles" **love** to make decisions for themselves, **and** for everyone else if possible.

It is important to realize however, that any decision the "Eagle" makes will have something in it for him/her - even if it's only increased esteem from the followers. "Eagles" are also the best "politicians." They tend to reach the top of the political hierarchy first and rarely hesitate to step on others to get there. Associates respect and fear them, often with little love lost.

True "Eagles" have a life history of radically changing everything and everyone with whom they come in contact. If there is no problem to deal with, the "Eagle" will create one!

When they're in leadership roles (assuming they're qualified for the position), they're capable of making massive contributions to the organisation fortunate enough to have them. They can be the true change agents with a level of energy and focus that is enviable to all.

Character indicators
Quick character indicators of the Eagle personality are:
~ The directness of their approach - they say what they mean, as **they** see it, and with little embellishment.

~ One track minds - they rarely deviate from the point that they're wanting to make

~ Their rate of speech - typically very fast

~ Tone of voice - firm, authoritative

~ The controlling nature of their conversation - they tend to tell rather than ask

~ Their verbal communication - they speak with authority, and warmth is an extremely rare commodity. Attempts to **appear** caring may come across as being patronising and condescending

~ High competitiveness in all they do

~ Little to no concern about the feelings of others when they want something, and

~ Things **rapidly** reverting to the subjective if they aren't getting their way

Personal traits
Some of the more recognisable personal traits include:
~ They tend to be early arrivers (they like to be first). Alternatively, they'll arrive late - just to show that they have the authority to come and go as they please

- ~ Their impatience soon leads to "fidgeting" when things are taking too long
- ~ They don't think twice about interrupting someone when what they have to say is "more important," and will often finish your sentences for you
- ~ They are "game players" and politicians
- ~ Interestingly, they like telling jokes
- ~ They use the "power handshake" where their hand is presented palm downwards
- ~ They **HATE** losing, and can even go so far as to throw a tantrum when they do, and
- ~ They dislike detail

Their verbal communications will be:
Authoritative, louder, fast paced with little to no warmth, confident with statements like
- ~ What I want to know is...
- ~ We need to escalate this...
- ~ Do it now...
- ~ ASAP
- ~ You can call me at...
- ~ The bottom line is...
- ~ How long is this going to take?
- ~ Look I don't have a lot of time...
- ~ I want to speak to the Manager
- ~ I expect...
- ~ This is not good enough...
- ~ No that won't work for me...

Primary turn on
The primary turn on for the Eagle personality is control and results. To make an Eagle happy - give them the reins and give them results.

Fear

The greatest fear of the "Eagle" personality is to be taken advantage of by someone "lesser" than them. They fear loss of control but to be taken advantage of - especially with public knowledge (i.e. loss of face), is their worst nightmare.

Appearance

"Eagle's" are very image conscious. Name brands are preferred clothing and if they can afford it, they will go for "tailor made." Generally their clothes are "smart conservative" but they will deviate slightly "if everyone else is doing it." They like expensive brief cases - leather only of course, and will always have an expensive pen at the ready. An expensive watch will be displayed whenever appropriate as they "check on the time."

Women go for suits with tailored cuts and conservative colours. They generally wear only basic jewellery but what they do wear will be 18 carat and expensive. Make-up is usually very discreet, and nails are usually well manicured and short. The higher the Eagle characteristic, the more likely medium heels will be worn as opposed to high heels.

Body language

One of the most notable things about the "Eagle" is the way they seem to be composed - all the time. Other pointers include:

~ Movement - they usually move purposefully even when merely going to the toilet

~ Eyes - their gaze can be very penetrating - as if they're trying to look right inside and analyse you, so they will know what makes you tick

~ When angry – they are masters of the "jabbing finger"

~ Mouth - often very tight, almost tense in appearance, and

~ They're often athletic in build. Their competitiveness often leads them to play sports like squash as well as the "expected" golf.

Office

The "Eagle office tends to be full of status symbols and will be as large as can be justified. An oversized desk, full couch, and designer furniture will be evident subject only to budget. Walls will be decorated with certificates of education and/or achievement, along with trophies and an occasional photograph of the incumbent.

"Eagles" like to have lots of "plastic" with them, with membership cards for all the private clubs and Frequent Flyer programs. If they are into technology, it's important to sport the latest in electronic gadgetry.

Building rapport, Dealing with, the "Eagle"

If you don't want to be "creamed" by an Eagle it is important that you **do**:

~ Speak with firm confidence

~ Give impressions of efficiency by emphasis on how you "get things done"

~ Focus on "the bottom line"

~ Don't waste time

~ Give them promises of results

~ Be direct and candid in your approach

~ Use positive statements

~ Be concise

~ Be prepared and I **mean** prepared - don't leave **anything** to chance and don't just look at "**your**" side - things will be **far** less confrontational if you show understanding (and acceptance) for their side too

~ Maintain emotional control - a common strategy of the "Eagle" is to get the other person emotional and when this has been achieved, you will almost invariably lose. Another Eagle I knew would ask Sales people to send detailed information to him prior to meeting with them. Then, when they met he would say – "Well I didn't lose any sleep to excitement over this meeting and I didn't have time to read this, so you've got 60 seconds to tell me why I should listen to you..."

~ In true negotiating style - give them some things they can say "No" to early in the piece, as they become far more tractable, when they think they're comfortably ahead

~ Show interest in them - what they do, their successes, etc.

~ Name drop - especially where they can get the impression that you may be able to help with their career

- Use words such as control, power, authority, command, success, speed, efficiency, improve, challenge, take over, dominate, etc. in your conversation

- Make sure they can see something in it for them, in anything you suggest,

- Negotiate - the Eagle rarely **ever** accepts the first offer. Their competitive nature **demands** that they try to get a reduction or something free with their purchase

- Admit immediately if you're unsure about an answer. The confidence and honesty indicated by this, will gain their respect

- Make sure you give the "Eagle" your total attention. It drives them nuts when they don't think you're listening

- Let them feel that they have control

- Don't be afraid to talk (briefly) about yourself and your success. They like to think they're dealing with successful people

- Make statements that suggest that it is not going to involve any effort on their part, and

- Present it as the best way to do it - the one that will get the best/fastest results

Appreciate that the "Eagle" has little loyalty to anyone or anything but him/herself. Their loyalty goes to the object, article, service that they feel presents them in the best light.

Lead to a decision
The following "lead ins" will assist you in closing your conversation or sale with an "Eagle:"

- With the improved results...

- Making a decision on this...

- I guess you will want to move quickly on this...

- With us taking care of all the detail stuff...

- It seems the challenge for you will...

- This will allow you more time for the important things...

- You will know exactly where you are...

- You will have total control...

~ This will get things moving

~ Your blockages will be a thing of the past...

Under stress
Under stress, typically, the "Eagle" personality will dictate, become very loud and demanding, and will potentially lash out at all and sundry.

When the "Eagle" is under stress they may appear:
~ More restless

~ Hyper critical

~ More blunt

~ More intrusive

~ Even more uncooperative

~ Irritable, and

~ More aggressive

Helping them
If you hope to quickly bring them back to productivity they will need:
~ Control of situation and self

~ A clear plan that they can work towards

~ Tangible evidence of progress

~ A fast pace for reaching goals, and

~ Directness, clarity and conciseness in your communication

Using them as a sounding board – (coming to them with problems **and** solutions) can also help

Do Not:
You will lose them if you:
~ Give vague answers

~ Waffle

~ Be long winded

~ Indicate even the slightest uncertainty

~ Give any indication that you are intimidated by them, or

~ Go over their head unless there is absolutely no other way

One Other - Kea (Creative)

General comment

There **is** another personality that merits mention but not the detail entered into so far. I say this only because there aren't so many people who truly fit this category which is probably best represented, by the Kea. This bird is native to New Zealand, and is the wackiest bird you can imagine. They are curious, incredibly intelligent, and are renowned for stripping everything that can sensibly be removed from a car, in less time than you would believe.

I remember my previous father-in-law (an avid hunter) coming back from hunting elk one day - still in tears from laughing. Apparently he had been up in the Alps and was carefully lining his gun up on a stag that was just coming out from some trees below. Before he could pull the trigger, a Kea landed on the end of the gun with its head upside down as it looked up the hole of the barrel, trying to see what was in there.

"Keas" are the right brainers, creative, "space cadets," who seem to operate on another plane.

They're often **extremely** intelligent with very high IQ's, they get bored quickly (**instantly** it would seem at times), and "focus" has the same effect on them as alien abductions on most other people. They're the "free spirits" of society and do not process information in the manner that the other personality types do. They're creative, conceptual, and often **extremely** intuitive, with decisions based on "feel" rather than logic.

Detail is something that is almost impossible for the "Kea" personality. They **can** do it but it is so unnatural to them that their very survival is at risk if forced to focus on it for too long. "Keas" are far more interested in ideas than in "practical" matters and often have memories like sieves. Unless it is something that interests them, they will often have forgotten it immediately you have finished telling them

They are often very "spiritual" people as opposed to religious.

Character indicators

People with the "Kea" personality type can be recognised by:

~ Their lack of organisation

~ Their inability to focus on anything for any amount of time

~ Their "bubbly" natures

~ The fact that nothing seems to bother them for long

~ Their natural positivity, and

~ Their clothes

Personal traits

Some of the more recognisable personal traits of the "Kea" include:

~ Spontaneity

~ They're forever "losing" things (but not worrying about it)

~ Rebellion against anything that tries to "put them in a box"

~ Disorganisation

~ They tend to be day dreamers

~ Having spoken to them about something they will often respond with something that seems as far removed as ice cream from curry, and

~ Apparent fickleness as they flit from one thing/person to another

They will typically use action words/statements like:

The following words/statements will appear often in the conversation of a "Kea" personality:

~ Why?

~ What if...

~ Experiment...

~ Why don't we...

~ Try...

~ Incredible...

~ Amazing...

~ Create...

~ Develop...

~ Paperwork is a waste of time...

- ~ Oh it will be here somewhere...

- ~ I haven't seen that in ages

- ~ He hasn't had an original idea in years...

- ~ Do we have to...?

- ~ Oh God...

Primary turn on
The primary turn on for the "Kea" is freedom - to be, to do, and to play.

Fear
The greatest fear of the "Kea" personality is to have their wings clipped - to be restricted in a situation where they have to do the same repetitive task over and over.

Appearance
The male "Kea" personality tends to dress casual to the point of looking dishevelled. They often look like they have just got out of bed, and ironing is one of those things they just don't understand, about what "other" people do. It is easy to get the impression that they're colour-blind with the mix of colours they will wear.

They see absolutely nothing wrong with wearing shorts and sandals when everyone else is in long trousers and shoes, or different coloured socks at the same time. In the extreme however, they may go to the latest in fashion and wear those items that were meant for catwalks but never intended to be sold to the public. They will often sport beards and ponytails, and are often seen unshaven, even where they don't have a beard.

Female "Keas" love purples, blues, yellows, browns and greens - preferably the brighter shades. They can be seen in Tee shirts, bra-less, and in long flowing skirts, which again don't often see an iron. Hair is often at risk of not seeing a comb - usually long and flowing, perhaps in plaits or braided in the African style, and they are more likely than most to be sporting a flower in the hair. Flat comfortable footwear is their preference.

Alternatively, they will look like something straight out of the latest fashion magazine, the more frilly – the better.

212

Body language

Typical body language indicators of the "Kea" personality include:

~ An apparent ability to defy gravity as they "float" along

~ Wandering eyes even when you are trying to hold their attention, and

~ Animated gestures

Office

Absolutely **no** one can make as big a mess of an office as a "Kea" personality. Pictures will often be of whales or dolphins or abstract paintings - none of which will be hung straight.

Building Rapport, Dealing with, the "Kea" personality

If you want to build rapport with or "sell" to the "Kea" personality then:

~ Talk fast - remember they bore easily

~ Crack a (good) joke if possible - they love to laugh

~ Demonstrate all the bells and whistles (with enthusiasm)

~ If possible show what is unique to your product or service

~ Compliment the "Kea's" quick uptake

~ Talk about the environmentally kind elements of your product

~ Talk about "new" and "revolutionary," and

~ Move to agreement quickly - they're spontaneous people

Leading them to a decision...

Lead in's to closing for the "Kea" personality might follow the lines of...

~ Well I don't want to take up too much of your time - shall we...

~ How do you feel about the concept...?

~ Can you see how this will take you to...?

~ Imagine the results...

~ Picture yourself...

Do not (you will lose them if):

~ You get too detailed

~ You move too slowly, or if

~ You try to "tie them down"

COMPATIBILITY ISSUES BETWEEN THE PERSONALITY STYLES

Note that all of the Personalities are most comfortable with those of their own kind. With the others there will always varying degrees of incompatibility.

MONKEY

Monkey/Owl - The "Owl" personality is the one that throws the "Monkey." Their attention to detail, their aloofness and their slow pace (in the "Monkey's" perception) just drives the "Monkey" nuts.

Monkey/Retriever
The "Retriever" is the favourite of the "Monkey" because of their nurturing nature, and their caring. They appreciate the respect that the Retriever shows for them, but they struggle somewhat with their desire for detail, and their slow pace. The "Kea" is a close second as favourite.

Monkey/Eagle
The Monkey is the style that is least intimidated by the Eagle. They like their pace and their decisiveness, but may be concerned with their lack of caring.

Monkey/Kea
The "Kea" absolutely delights and fascinates the "Monkey." Their intellect, their free spirit and their ability to be as happy alone as they are amongst other people, is something the "Monkey" is in awe of.

OWL

Owl/Monkey/Kea - The "Monkey" and the "Kea" personalities are the ones that the Owl has the most difficulty with. The "flamboyance" of the "Monkey," the speed they operate at, and their "touchy-feeliness" throw the Owl. The inability of the "Kea" to sit still and their lack of attention to detail irritates the "Owl" something terrible.

Owl/Retriever

The "Owl" gets along quite well with the "Retriever," becoming uncomfortable only with their tendency to be emotional, and their need to be with other people.

Owl/Eagle
The "Owl" appreciates the "Eagle's" conciseness and coldness. The main areas of discomfort come from the "Eagle's" pace, their love of change, their lack of attention to detail, and what the "Owl" perceives as their lack of concern over unfairness at times.

RETRIEVER

Retriever/Monkey - the "Monkey" is the style that the Retriever is most comfortable with because they're the people the "Retriever" aspires to be. They appreciate the caring aspect of the "Monkey" and to be as confident amongst people as the "Monkey" is, is the stuff of dreams for the "Retriever."

Their only concerns come from the "Monkey's" apparent lack of discipline, their fast pace, their lack of attention to detail, and their love of change.

Retriever/Owl – while the "Retriever" appreciates the "Owl's" slower pace and attention to detail, they are made uncomfortable by their aloofness, and lack of warmth.

Retriever/Eagle - no one bothers the "Retriever" more than the "Eagle." They admire their decisiveness but are intimidated by it as well, and the thing that disturbs the Retriever most is the apparent lack of caring. They also struggle with the "Eagle's" pace, and their seeming love of conflict. The typical reaction of the "Retriever" in the presence of the "Eagle" is to withdraw, if they can't physically just disappear.

Retriever/Kea
The Retriever's biggest problem with the "Kea" is that they can't figure them out. They seem to be very caring but they never sit still long enough to really find out, and they seem to have a complete disdain for detail and discipline.

EAGLE

Eagle/Monkey/Owl

Outside of other "Eagles," the "Eagle" probably comes closest to a level of compatibility with the "Monkey" and/or the "Owl" depending on circumstances at the time. They like the fast pace and love of change of the Monkey, they respect their ability to get along with others, and especially, their persuasiveness. They enjoy the "Owl's" lack of emotion and their intelligence, but have difficulty with their indecisiveness, and their slow pace.

Eagle/Retriever - The "Eagle" has little to no respect for the "Retriever" whom they regard as "weak." They find the "Retriever" to be painfully emotional, and painfully slow.

Eagle/Kea - the "Kea" is the one that drives "Eagles" crazy. Their tendency to flit from one thing to another with no apparent organization, and their lack of respect for authority and discipline, makes "Eagles" want to scream!

KEA

Kea/Monkey

"Keas" get along fine with "Monkeys" – they love their spontaneity, their pace, their caring, and their love of "fun."

Kea/Owl

The "Kea" just doesn't bother him/herself with "Owls" – they are too slow and boring, and they don't seem to have any fun.

Kea/Retriever

The "Kea" is mildly intrigued by the "Retriever" – they seem like nice people – it just takes too long to get to know them.

Kea/Eagle

The "Kea" is not intimidated by the "Eagle" but they don't like them. They're too bossy, seem to want everyone in a cage, are "cold" personalities, and just no fun.

COMBINATIONS:

As I said earlier, you will rarely meet anyone who totally fits any one category and if you do - let's hope it's not an eagle. The secondary element in their profile will help to tone down the primary style, and often make them better people for it.

Quick Recognition

When you meet another person, the first thing you will notice is that you "warm" to them, or you don't. The next thing you will tend to notice is their pace – fast or slower.

Print and read "**More Quick Id**" and you will be on your way to defining the personalities of other people, almost as soon as you meet them.

IMPROVING RELATIONSHIPS

If you hope to improve your ability to get along with the other personality styles then you need to get into their world, before trying to bring them into yours.

MONKEY

Monkey/Owl

If you want to improve relations with the "Owl" then you must **slow down**, drop the "warm fuzzies" that come so natural to you, and at least **try** to accept a little more detail.

Monkey /Retriever

While you don't have a lot of problems with the "Retriever," slowing down and accepting a little more detail will improve things even further here.

Monkey/Eagle

The only thing needed from the "Eagle" to improve relations is respect. Be more decisive, and stand up for yourself more.

Monkey/Kea

No changes are needed here.

OWL

Owl/Monkey

If you are to have **any** kind of relationship with the "Monkey" you **must** speed up, give away some of your detail, and try to show some interest in them as people (enter into some "small-talk" with them).

Owl/Retriever

The only incompatibility with the "Retriever" is your seeming lack of "warmth." Lighten up and don't be so afraid of showing that you really do care.

Owl/Eagle
To gain more respect from the "Eagle," you absolutely **must** speed up, be prepared to make a decision even if it is the wrong one, and cut down on detail.

Owl/Kea
The changes here may just be too great for you – you know the incompatibilities – do the best you can.

RETRIEVER

Retriever/Monkey
Not a lot of problems here – just speed things up a bit, don't be so detailed, and all should go well.

Retriever/Owl
Not a lot of problems here either – just watch your emotions and keep sentimentality in check.

Retriever/Eagle
To have any chance of a relationship with the "Eagle" you absolutely **must** "toughen up." Don't allow things to become personal, **speed up**, drop some of the detail, and make a decision – wrong or otherwise. Most importantly – prepare for the meeting – know what you want, why you want it, why it is important, how it is going to help the "Eagle" look good, and what compromises you are willing to accept (or not).

Retriever/Kea
Just be prepared to speed up – don't be so serious, and drop the detail.

EAGLE
Eagle/Monkey
Relationships here should not be too troublesome anyway. To improve – show a little more respect, and don't be so cold.

Eagle/Owl

218

Once again relationships here should be fairly reasonable – slowing down and allowing some more detail than you are used to, would definitely help though.

Eagle/Retriever

Don't be such a bully. Slow down, don't get personal, and be willing to accept a little more detail. Praising a job well done, would also go a long way here.

Eagle/Kea

The only way you are going to work with the Kea is to respect that you will never control them, enjoy their genuine brilliance, and deal with them only when you have to.

KEA

Kea/Monkey

No real changes needed here

Kea/Owl

This one is not likely ever to work – you can see the areas of incompatibility – do the best you can.

Kea/Retriever

Just slow down and listen.

Kea/Eagle

If you can accommodate the "Eagle's" ego – you'll be fine here.

Exercise:

1. What is your main personality type and what is your supporting type.

2. List the most important people to you (personal & work). Using the "More Quick Id," note what you assess their primary and supporting styles as being, alongside of their name.

3. What are the primary indicators leading you to believe the people match the styles you have chosen?

4. What will you do to enhance your relationships with each of those people?

Chapter 19

BEING THE BEST (PERSON) YOU CAN BE
A summary of the program so far with some extremely valuable additional pointers

Some qualities of the greatest human beings include - they:
~ Are **genuine**

~ Are **honest** and act with **integrity**

~ Are **proud** of themselves (with good reason)

~ Are **confident**

~ Have **empathy** for their other people

~ Are **unaffected by** the negatives faced by other people

~ **Know what they want** and go after it with a plan

~ **Face** their fears and overcome them

~ **Do what they say** they will do – when they said they would do it

~ Are **enthusiastic**

~ They **actively** try to see the other person's point of view

~ Don't believe in **failure**

~ **Never** make **decisions** for other people

~ Don't **allow** complacency

~ They set goals and work to achieve them, and

~ They seek **learning** opportunities the whole of their lives

Genuine - if you're not **genuine** in your approach to **all** of these qualities and tools, you will **never** be truly great, in **anything** that you do. Something almost all people detest is to be patronised. Don't do it.

Honesty/integrity - **dis**honesty will almost **always** catch up with you; it's just not worth it. You have to have too good a memory to be a successful liar, and it becomes a terrible task remembering whom you've told what to. People will not always **like** your honesty but they will always **respect** it.

Answer the question "Who would **YOU** rather deal with - someone you like but can't trust, or someone you don't necessarily **like** but whom you can always depend on?" It's interesting that salespeople use honesty and integrity in the same sentence time and again yet when asked what the difference is, few have the answer. What do you think?

Honesty is telling the truth – integrity goes a step beyond that – it is "doing the right thing by others." So if we meet on a mountain path and you ask – "Does this path go all the way to the top" (and it does) and I answer "Yes" – I have been honest with you. Integrity however might change the answer to "Yes it does but a 60 metre section has subsided about 800 metres up the mountain, and I'm not sure if you have the equipment to get around that."

Pride – the truly great people are **proud** of who they are. They **don't** however, look down on other people - it's a personal thing.

Confidence - they believe implicitly in their ability to help others to improve their businesses or lives. They **know** their worth.

Empathy - truly great people **lead** people with care and concern for their well-being. They don't push. They totally understand the difference between empathy and sympathy. What do they mean to you?

*(If you empathise with someone, you appreciate and care about their difficulty but you **don't make it yours**.) You **demonstrate** your caring, but you don't allow their problems to weigh you down because if you do, it may stop you from selling something or saying something for example, that would have helped to get them out of their mess.*

Unaffected - the truly great people know they can't solve the problems of the world, **so they don't concern themselves with them.**

Quote: *"Worry is like a rocking chair - it keeps you occupied but doesn't get you very far." Originator unknown.* You will meet with a host of negative situations in your life and career and in order to avoid being brought down by them; you **have** to leave them "outside."

Discussion - *if someone brought you a package and you knew that what was inside was a virus that had the potential to destroy you and your family - would you take it into your home?*

*If your answer was "No," then why do you do that with problems that are not yours? Taking on other people's problems can do **all** of those things, as effectively as any virus.*

*If you come across a person who has fallen into a quicksand pit, would you agree that the best way to help them is to jump in too? No? So what **would** you do? Again - why not do that with their problems?*

Know what they want - all truly great people are very clear on what is important to them - they know what they want out of life, and they're prepared to **go out and get it.** Great people get what they want on **merit** though - not on the backs of other people.

Fear – the truly great people of this world **face** their fear & **overcome** it where most people spend their lives hiding it from others, and most times from themselves as well. Fear and worry go almost hand in hand and worry is perhaps the most insane emotion of all. Statistics show that worrying has never solved a single problem, in the history of the planet - **EVER**. It **does** make you sick, and it **can** make you pretty unpleasant to be around - so if that's what you want out of life, then go ahead and worry I guess.

Do what they say they will do – false promises will cause people to lose respect for you faster than a greyhound with a wasp under his tail. We can't always do what we said we would do – when we said we would do it, because circumstances change. When things change however, you have nothing to lose and everything to gain, by simply advising people of the delay or whatever. People in Management **especially**, need to learn this fact.

Enthusiasm - truly great people carry their own sunshine with them. They are genuinely enthusiastic about **life**, their **job, and** themselves because they actively look for the positives in all things. When times

222

are "bad," they may be even **more** enthusiastic, because they believe they can **change** that.

Failure - the truly great amongst us know there is no such thing as failure. *Remember my ant?*

Decisions - no great person falls into the trap of making decisions for other people. An example of what I am talking about here, might go like this... You are feeling really down one day and there is an acquaintance of yours who always lifts you up when you are in his or her company. You think, "Maybe I should give them a call" and then in comes the ego talk – blah bah blah... "Oh no they would want to hear from me, they don't want to hear about my problems, they hardly even know me, they're probably busy right now..." and so on.

You have just made a decision for that other person that is not your right to make. Maybe they are sitting at home bored, thinking – "Gee I wish someone would give me a call and suggest going for a walk or... anything..." and you have just denied them that break by "deciding" on their behalf that they wouldn't want to see you. Can you see the arrogance in that?

Complacency – complacency is avoided at all costs by the truly great, because they know that next to ego, no other thing contributes more, to our losing or missing out on some of the most important experiences of our lives.

Learning – truly great people know one of the most important aspects of this life, is the learning that we take out of it. They take every opportunity to extend their knowledge – knowing that it will help to make them a better person.

Most importantly of all though - **IF YOU WANT TO BE A TRULY GREAT PERSON TOO:**

Be **CONSCIOUSLY** great **ALL the time!!** We have somehow allowed ourselves to be fooled into thinking that we have three separate lives – our work life, our personal life and our social life. If that were true, then after the worst possible day at work, you would make the "going home switch" and go home without a care in the world and vice versa.

Be **professional ALL THE TIME!!** Once again it is easier if you do it **all** the time. If you're one of these people who are professional when you know there are important people about but let it all hang out when there aren't, one day you're sure to get caught. When you go to that bar or restaurant and make a fool of yourself you can almost **bet** there will be a person that you are going to want to impress at some time in your life - sitting somewhere close by, wondering "who on earth is that idiot." Don't do it!

Treat **EVERYONE** around you as if they were going to be the most important person in your life one day - **ALL THE TIME!!** When you find yourself speaking to the person next to you in a manner that you would **never** use on someone "important," ask yourself is it any more appropriate than if the person **was** someone "important" - really?

You just never know who that person is married to, related to, or is just good friends with. You have no idea where you will meet them again, later in your life. So if you have just said a few things that you would **not** have said to someone "important," think about it. You could be losing more opportunities than you realise, without ever knowing why. It is a wise person who remembers the adage "be nice to people on the way up, because you never know who you'll meet again, on the way down."

UNDER commit and **OVER** deliver in **ALL** that you do.   People may **hate** having you tell them that you can't **possibly** get that job or whatever done till Wednesday - when in their perception, their whole world is going to end if you don't do it by Tuesday. But they **will** respect your honesty. When you **do** deliver on Wednesday they will respect you even more but if you actually **do** manage to do it on Tuesday or even better - Monday, they'll think you're the best thing since soft tissue.

Allow them to pressure you into saying that you **will** do it on Tuesday and **then** deliver on Wednesday, and you are dead meat as far as that prospect is concerned.

I have a thought for all of you who **really** are interested in improving yourselves and that is... **ALL** *people bring happiness into this world - some as they* **COME***, & some as they* **GO***. Originator unknown*. Give some thought to where **YOU** fit.

Understand true needs and base everything you do on this. Without an understanding of true needs, it is entirely possible to be walking all over people in your dealings with them, and not even realise you are doing it. If you trample on other people's needs whether consciously or **sub**consciously, then you will never, ever, rise to "Great Person" status.

UNDERSTAND – take time to understand the people you would like in your life. *(Seek to understand before attempting to be understood- a **great** relationship building concept).*

Find out about:
~ Their aspirations

~ What motivates them

~ Their goals

LISTEN!!! for those wonderful little words that people often use unconsciously that tell you **exactly**, what is important to them. References to cost, time, family, how busy they are; all of these things are giving you direction as to what is most important to them right now.
~ How much do you learn about other people when **YOU** are doing the talking? *Not a lot do you?*

~ How much do you learn about what is important to them, when **YOU** are doing the talking? *Not much again wouldn't you agree?*

~ How **INTERESTED** do you think the other person feels you are in them personally, when **YOU** are doing the talking? *Not very wouldn't you say?* So learn how to get **them** doing the talking! The saying that "all the world loves a lover" **may** be true, but it is **certainly** true that all the world loves a listener.

Why does everyone love a listener? Unfortunately we do have a compulsion to be the one doing the talking because from our school days and perhaps even earlier, we've been taught that the speaker is in charge! **"Don't interrupt** when I'm talking! **Listen** to me - I have important things to tell you (and therefore **I** am important)." Don't believe it. The **LISTENER** holds **ALL** the aces.

You have to speak **SOMETIME** however, so when you do - how do you get the other person to **want** to listen?

- ~ Appear to have at least one lobe to your brain - say something intelligent (or funny).

- ~ Give them a **reason** to listen to you - say something that will interest them

- ~ Avoid "ahs, uhmms" and "like"

- ~ Speak **clearly** & ensure that the other party can hear

- ~ Paint **pictures** with your words. *(Right brain people find it difficult to relate to words, and people are more likely to be convinced by an emotional approach)*

- ~ **Vary** the tone of your voice

- ~ **ASK QUESTIONS**

- ~ Inject **humour** where appropriate *(but be **VERY** careful here, because it is unbelievably easy to offend)*

- ~ Ensure that the other party **understands** what you are saying - don't talk over their head

- ~ Ensure that what you are saying is **relevant** to **their** situation

- ~ **KNOW WHEN TO SHUT UP!!**

- ~ Don't be afraid to be **different**

C A R E!!

- ~ About the other person

- ~ About what is best for **them**

- ~ About your attitude, & how you present yourself, About how well you do your job

- ~ About the people who work with, & around you, and

- ~ Remember that **EVERY** time you are in contact with **any** human being **A SALE DOES TAKE PLACE!!** *The most basic sale on parting will be "Gee I really enjoyed meeting Jenny and I sure hope we get to spend some time together again" or... "I'd rather watch a four hour documentary on the mating of the South American tree snail, than spend five **minutes** in her company again!*

Take responsibility

One of the first things you were asked to do in this program was to take responsibility for at least 90% of what happens in your life from here on. That means – you take responsibility for **you**.

You are the only thing that you can reasonably be expected to take responsibility for. You should **act** responsibly towards everyone and everything in your life but you cannot **take** responsibility, for anything that you don't have minute-by-minute control over.

Think about it! The ego just **loves** to make us feel responsible for that which we cannot be responsible for. There is no more perfect ground, for personal abuse.

Chapter 20

ALIGNMENT

Introduction

If we are to truly live lives of value and fulfillment in this lifetime, it starts with alignment. When we are totally aligned at all levels with our Soul Purpose, we have the maximum "power" available to us in this consciousness, to achieve that which we set out to achieve. **Any** misalignment can rob you of more power than you could ever believe, and this can be demonstrated physically.

A great example might be to connect a hose to the very bottom of the biggest damn on earth. Interestingly, I only have to put a few kinks in that hose and all that you will get at the end, is a trickle. Anyone looking at the end of the hose (who doesn't know about the dam), will look at the trickle and tell you "There's no water in there" and yet if I was to take the kinks out, you'd probably be flying around through the air, trying to hold on.

We are no different and if you consider the "dam" that **we** are connected to – what do you think you could be doing in **your** life – if we took the kinks out of you?

Soul purpose:

If you don't know what your life/soul purpose is, then what **are** you aligned with, or to? In the absence of an understanding of your life's purpose, it is almost impossible to have a direction in life that is "meant for you," as each of your elements (heart, mind, body, etc) attempts to align to its **own** purpose.

Symptoms of a missing "life purpose" include:
~ Mental confusion

~ No direction

~ Little satisfaction

~ Poor health, and

~ Emotional discontent.

So what is **your** soul's purpose (why are you here in other words)?

This can be a toughie for many people because we are so out of alignment (and therefore "out of tune/touch" with our true selves), that the likelihood of discovering our life purpose, seems about as remote as flying to the moon without a spaceship.

Heart
Our heart is our soul connection. Unfortunately though, we often force the heart to align more closely to the head than the soul, and we wonder why we have so many emotional issues in our lives?
Indications of a heart head alignment include feelings of:

~   Guilt

~   Fear

~   Jealousy

~   Hatred

~   Loneliness, etc

Mind
Our mind is the "conscious" connection and via the ego – it tries to "run the show" entirely, putting us out of alignment with the body, ensuring that our actions are not aligned with what is in our hearts, and that our hearts are totally out of alignment with our life's purpose.

Unfortunately, we have given the mind the "Boss" title and as such, it dictates what we do, think, and feel.

Body
The body is the host that allows us to be here and yet we often treat it more as the enemy than as a friend, by...

~   Not giving it the **rest** that it needs

~   Not **exercising**, and

~   Putting "**stuff**" in and on it, that it was never designed to work with

Thank goodness the energy of the body does not change as quickly as the energy of thought, or we would find ourselves in **far** more trouble than we could imagine. The body **does** catch up eventually though and whatever is in your mind (or heart) will eventually surface in the body, in a variety of illnesses.

By way of example – think of the things that tend to "consume" our every thought and action:

~ Bitterness

~ Thoughts of revenge

~ Stress

~ Worry

~ Anxiety

~ Etc.

Allow yourself to be consumed by any **one** of these things, and eventually the body will follow – consuming **itself**, with cancer.

Actions
Our actions are often diametrically opposed to our purpose, our thinking, and our hearts.

For example:

~ We tell someone we love them; and then we treat them like something we picked up off the lawn - showering them with mental, emotional and sometimes, even physical abuse.

~ Alternatively – we loudly and proudly champion the need to take better care of the environment - but we work for a company that is renowned for its environmental unfriendliness.

~ We say "I love my body" as we fill it with Coke and fast food

~ We tell ourselves that we are valued and special individuals, yet we will often stay in abusive relationships where we are grossly undernourished in every way

~ We say we love this beautiful "Planet Earth" and yet we are in a race to destroy it...

~ Where is the alignment here?

Change
How do we **change** this? A wonderful question.

For some it may be a matter of stepping back (taking time out) and trying to reconnect to our soul energy.

For others it may be more appropriate to look at the results / consequences of our actions, and work back from there.

Alternatively, for some it may be more effective to go straight to the ego, and attack the issue there because the ego will be behind everything that is misaligned in our lives – everything else is a symptom.

Start

A great place to start is to ask the question, "What would I like people to say about me after I am gone?"

If you would like to think that people would have nice things to say about you – what would those nice statements include?

Alignment can start at either end. You can go the spiritual route, or you can start with your behaviour.

The spiritual route may involve:
~ Attempting to find your version of "God," evaluating what He/She would want of you and then working forward from there

~ Imagine yourself standing before your "God" and telling him/her what you achieved in your life. If you don't feel too comfortable with this then these is an obvious misalignment here – what do you need to change? Or,

~ Defining what a truly "good person" looks like to you (how would you expect such a person to behave in other words), and then working to align your own behaviour to that ideal.

Behaviour is the action that follows thoughts and feelings, so you can work back from there.

Whatever route you choose, in order to be truly aligned throughout your being, your behaviour/actions must match your thinking, which must match your heart, which must be attuned to whatever it is that you are here to achieve.

Your behaviour includes how you treat other people **and** yourself. Do you take care of your body externally and internally (exercise, good food, clean water, rest...)? **You** are so important in this equation –

we so often neglect ourselves in the process of taking care of others, and full alignment is not possible in this model.

Consider your thoughts – what do you feed your mind on? Are your thoughts positive – towards yourself and other people? Do you have your ego in control?

And what about your heart - do you find yourself suppressing your heart, or encouraging it, by listening and responding to your feelings? Do you allow yourself to love without restriction, or do you "keep the reins on" so you don't get hurt?

All of the tips and tools that you have learned here, should be applied to this alignment and when you do it, you will feel logarithmic increases in your personal power.

Finishing up...
Consider that *"The lighthouse has no way of understanding why the sea is so angry on any given day, but all it **needs** to understand – is that that is when it's light must shine brightest." Tom Grbich.*

As you will by now be aware - changing your life involves **far** more than just "visualising" all the wonderful things that you want **in** life as suggested by the so-called "Secret."

First
- Make yourself aware of the cause/s of all the "negative" thinking that led to the experiences in life that you would rather not have had, and then
- Teach yourself to be aware when your **current** thinking heads back in that direction, so that you can re-direct it immediately.

Second
Visualisation of the good things that you want in your life helps tremendously in manifesting those things as reality, and it is important to focus on the things you **do** want, not the things you **don't** want.

Just as when dieting – if you focus on all the things you **can't** eat, then the process will be a miserable one for you. Look only at the things that you **can** eat, and rejoice in them.

To emphasise that last statement – if your focus is split between the positive **and** the negative – you are going to have mixed results. Be aware of the negative but don't dwell there. All possible attention should be focused on the positive.

And finally, you absolutely **have** to be aligned in the whole process. You can visualise till the cows come home but if your thinking says "you don't deserve it," then it is unlikely ever to happen.

Example

If we go back to my colon issue – I had no shortage of negatives to distract me...

~ I was potentially going to die of gaseous gangrene

~ I was potentially going to bleed to death

~ I could not be operated on

~ There was no "magic pill" that was going to "fix" me

~ You can't heal that which is dead... and so on

I was **aware** of all of the negatives (how could I not be), but I focused my whole attention, energy, and visualisation on the positive...

~ The body has regenerative capabilities; and

~ I am living a normal live more than 3 years later.

Print a copy of the **Personal Evaluation-03** form and fill it out, then open your envelope and compare the changes again. As an ongoing measure of success – you can do this as many times as you want in the future.

Print the **Final Action Plan** and update all the things that you are planning to do from here, with dates alongside.

I look forward with all my heart, to hearing of your own personal success stories.

Common issues, and where to look for answers

Listed below are samples of the issues that people deal with every day and which may still arise having read the book. This is a quick reference guiding you to the chapters in the book that are most likely to contain an answer to the issue.

Issue	Comment	Chapter
I have problems with my **relationships** (parents, boss, kids, spouse, workmates)	Relationships define the quality of life for most people on the planet and the relationship you have with yourself is where it starts. There are many facets to this issue and all of the suggested chapters would need to be covered to truly address them.	3, 4, 5, 6, 7, 10, 12, 18, 19
How do I deal with **racism**?	Racism is mostly a factor of insecurity and/or misunderstanding. Avoiding them is the simplest solution – you have to appreciate that you are unlikely to be able to change them.	3, 7
How do I find my **life's path**?		16
How do I get the most out of life?	Learn what it is that you want most out of life then set goals for that achievement.	14, 16
How do I live up to the **expectations** of bosses, friends etc.?	Don't make their expectations yours. Appreciate that most times it is not possible to meet the expectations of others and maybe you shouldn't even try. Are the expectations realistic and are they achievable?	19
I have so many **problems** – what do I do?	Follow the proven problem solving process ...	11
I'm in a **rut** – how do I get out?	Revisit "What you want most out of life," set some goals, and if nothing else – work at being the best that you can be.	14, 16, 19
I'm overworked & **stressed** out –	The formula provided in chapter 8 should be revisited, then combine it	8, 9, 17

help me.	with the following chapters...	
I've had it with my **job** but I don't know what to do and I'm scared to quit.	Firstly – decide if it is the job, the boss, or the company that is the problem for you, then check out the following...	12, 13, 14, 15, 16, 17
I feel like I am **missing something** – what is it?		16
I need an **attitude** adjustment...	Check out why you feel your attitude is not contributing positively to your life, revisit the "Behaviour cycle" in chapter one and... take it from there.	1, 12, 13, 14
I need to **relax** and smell the roses – how do I make myself do it?	Check out the chapters suggested here and then ask, "If I knew I wasn't going to be here next week – how would I spend that time" – then **do** it.	7, 8, 17
There are many questions that could be asked on the emotional **needs chart** such as –"I don't feel appreciated or respected"...	The "Needs chart" provides you with a wonderful opportunity to understand which of your "need tanks" are depleted. This information can then be used to formulate a plan as to how you are going to change that. How you are treated by others is almost always a consequence of how they judge you, and how they judge you will almost always be a result of your behaviour.	1, 7
What does **EGO** mean?	Ego is most commonly mistaken as pride but it has so many more faces than that. At the very least it is **false** pride. Ego ultimately is the opinion you have of yourself.	3
What does it mean to be **successful**?	Success means so many different things to different people but ultimately perhaps, it is what people say about you over your grave, about what kind of person you were.	15
What is **love**?	Perhaps the simplest & most complex topic on the planet. Read chapter 10	10

	to decide for yourself but to me, it is the desire to assist those who are most important to you, to experience the greatest personal freedom & joy that this world can provide.	
Why does **love** so often result in pain?	Because we don't understand it, and therefore place expectations on it. It is the ego's absolutely favourite playground because of the impact it can have.	10
What is my **purpose**?	I believe it is to learn, to love and be loved, and to enjoy (have fun).	
Why do you say **awareness** is the most powerful tool?	With total awareness, you would always be in the right place at the right time and never in the wrong place at the wrong time. Awareness provides you with the ultimate choice.	
What is the difference between balance & **alignment**?	Balance is an inert state – alignment is direction – free from deviation or distraction.	
How do I deal with all the **"negative talk"** in my head?	Appreciate that it is just the "ego" doing its thing again and learn to deal with it...	3
How do I leave my **past** (baggage) behind and move to my ideal life?	Learn to disempower it. Unlike computers, our memories cannot be erased except by serious brain injury. So your "baggage" will never leave you - but you can **certainly** take its power away.	3
Will I ever truly find **happiness**?	Happiness cannot choose you – you have to choose it and when you do... yes you absolutely **can** be truly happy. The greatest contributor to **un**happiness is the ego...	3
How do I make sure I don't pass on my negative crap to my children?	Learn to precede all words and actions by the question, "Is this action or are these words likely to bring a positive result" (or consequence), and proceed accordingly.	3

Made in the USA
Charleston, SC
10 December 2014